FINDERS, KEEPERS

FINDERS, KEEPERS

ROSAMOND WOLFF PURCELL & STEPHEN JAY GOULD

EIGHT COLLECTORS

W · W · NORTON & COMPANY · NEW YORK · LONDON

Printed in Japan.

The text of this book is composed in Garamond #3,
with the display set in Centaur.
Composition by Kennedy Typographers.
Manufacturing by Dai Nippon Printing Co., Ltd., Tokyo, Japan.
Book design by Guenet Abraham.

First Edition
Library of Congress Cataloging-in-Publication Data

Purcell, Rosamond Wolff.
Finders, keepers : eight collectors / Rosamond Wolff Purcell &
Stephen Jay Gould.
p.   cm.
1. Collectors and collecting.   I. Gould, Stephen Jay.
II. Title
AM231.P87   1991
790.1'32—dc20   91-21055

ISBN 0-393-03054-7
W. W. Norton & Company, Inc.
500 Fifth Avenue, New York, N.Y. 10110
W. W. Norton & Company, Ltd.
10 Coptic Street, London WC1A 1PU

1 2 3 4 5 6 7 8 9 0

In memory of Robert Lee Wolff, collector extraordinaire,
and for Frank Lombardi, curator extraordinaire.

CONTENTS

INTRODUCTION

Thoughts of Britain may still inspire a vision of elaborate pomp and circumstance, at least when we consider such largely irrelevant but highly visible institutions as the monarchy. But the British version of our common language often shows the opposite trait of simple, plain meaning, where we favor the unnecessarily elaborate or obscure. In England, elevators are lifts, apartments are flats, and escalators are moving stairs. In America, a person in charge of a museum collection is a "curator," directly from the Latin for manager, or superintendent. (I am, for example and by official title, curator of invertebrate paleontology at Harvard's Museum of Comparative Zoology.) In Britain, my counterpart is, simply and equally officially, a "keeper." This book is a testimony of praise for the world's keepers, in this noble sense of guardian for natural treasures.

Of all nature's glories, none surpasses the stunning variety of myriad objects produced along the countless twigs of several billion years in life's evolutionary tree. Since art imitates life, we not only feel the urge to gather these objects into collections, but we do our gathering in modes and styles every bit as diverse as the items that we find and keep.

In planning this book on collectors and their quarries, we did not explicitly chart a preconceived range of diversity in times, places, social statuses, or objects. We simply chose places and people that compelled our attention for the fascination of objects gathered and contained. Yet the result, though organically meandering in execution, has the natural coherence of maximal diversity under the common rubric of passion for collecting.

Consider the range of our people in time, temperament, and status. They span more than 300 years, from the mannered baroque collections of Agostino Scilla, Frederik Ruysch, and Peter the Great to the matter-of-fact taxonomic gatherings of a twentieth-century Rothschild and Van Heurn. We run the gamut of social status from the most powerful of monarchs (Peter the Great) and wealthiest of financiers (Lord Rothschild) to amateurs surviving on the sale of local fossils (Mary Anning). Our cast includes madmen (Thomas Hawkins) and the most gentle of stereotypical museum labelers (Van Heurn); expansive charmers and entrepreneurs of science (Agassiz) and dyspeptic recluses who locked their objects from public view (Dubois). Our collectors worked throughout the world, from gathering domestic pigs and moles in their own backyards (Van Heurn), mounting expeditions to the most isolated regions of New Guinea in search of birds of paradise (Rothschild), even to serving as the only Western naturalist in a nation that confined all Europeans to an artificial island connected by a narrow causeway to Nagasaki (von Siebold in Japan under the Tokugawa shogunate).

Yet, amidst all this diversity, our collectors do hold one trait in common—probably the only feature that distinguishes people of true accomplishment, and that should serve as an inspiration to every human being of good will. They all believed passionately in the value of their work; they were driven, sometimes at the cost of life or sanity, by this conviction, this urge to collect, to bring part of a limitless diversity into an orbit of personal or public appreciation. In an age of passivity, where Walkman and television bring so much to us and demand so little in return, we must grasp the engaging passion of these collectors. And we must also remember that passion, for all its public and private joys, literally means suffering. The costs of engagement are high, but we must pay the price of our uniquely evolved consciousness. Better Socrates dissatisfied, as Mill said, than a pig satisfied. In any case, we have no choice.

The passion for collecting is a full-time job, a kind of blessed obsession. "Behold, he that keepeth Israel shall neither slumber nor sleep." And if we flip to the next page of the Bible, from this Psalm 121 to Psalm 127, the *Nisi Dominus*, we learn the true meaning of consecration. The form of the building, even the objects inside, count for nothing unless the intent be right. And here, for all their diversity, for all the dubious traits of their complex lives, our collectors may rest assured that they have been weighed in the balance and found worthy: "Except the Lord build the house, they labor in vain that build it; except the Lord keep the city, the watchman waketh but in vain."

FINDERS, KEEPERS

1 DUTCH TREAT: PETER THE GREAT AND FREDERIK RUYSCH

Our metaphors proclaim that we must build both upward and slowly—from little acorns—if we wish to impart strength and stability to any institution. But sometimes a perceived backwardness inspires a top-down approach—more chancy to be sure, but not without hope if inspired by adequate vision and wealth. As Peter the Great lay dying in 1725, he finally completed his plans to launch an Academy of Sciences on Western European models. Advisors criticized his plan to include a university, arguing that "there is no one to learn," for Russia had no secondary schools. Peter, aware of his impending end, replied:

> I have to harvest big stocks, but I have no mill; and there is not enough water close by. . . . But there is water enough at a distance; only I shall not have time to make a canal, for the length of my life is uncertain. Therefore, I am building the mill first and have only given orders for the canal to be begun, which will better force my successors to bring water to the completed mill.

Russia has often taken this top-down route, as rulers tried to use her vast spaces and natural wealth to leapfrog over the bonds of tradition or the thrall of serfdom. Many of our stereotypical images of this nation—from Peter personally cutting off the beards of his boyars and imposing western dress at court, to Stalin's forced industrialization and collectivization—embody this imposing theme.

We can find no better example of this distinctively Russian (and frequently Romanov) solution than the building of collections in arts and natural history. Catherine the Great (reigned 1762–1796), Peter's resolute and immensely talented granddaughter-in-law, brought the art of sudden acquisition to its apogee. She built the Hermitage in Peter's pristine capital of St. Petersburg and stocked her new art museum with mass purchases. In 1764, she bought 255 paintings from Frederick II of Prussia who, impoverished by the Seven Years' War, willingly sold Hals and Rembrandt to replenish the royal treasury. In 1779, she purchased more than 200 paintings from the estate of Sir Robert Walpole, prime minister to George I and George II; Parliament protested vigorously, but the sale went forward. When Catherine died in 1796, her collection stood just shy of 4,000 paintings.

Peter the Great was Catherine's prototype in the allied realm of natural history. Previous tsars had accumulated various bits and pieces from Europe, so Peter inherited a small and motley group of items, dating from Ivan the Terrible (mid to late sixteenth century) and including a "sea unicorn" (a narwhal's tooth) purchased by his father, Tsar Alexis. But Peter built a great collection by his own will and according to his own tastes. And, whereas Catherine worked almost exclusively by the former option of the contrast "buy or build," Peter balanced the two approaches by shaping, making, gathering, entreating, learning, and cultivating—as well as by unleashing the wealth of the Romanovs.

I have always been wary of epithets frequently attached to the names of monarchs. I am willing to believe Pepin the Short, or Charles the Bald (823–877), the Bad (1332–1387), the Fat (839–888), and the Simple (879–929), for these traits have never been much honored.

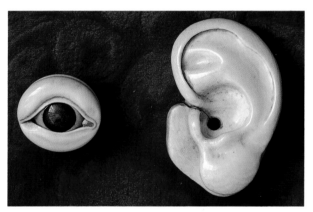

1. Ear and eye (13 parts, glass, antler bone, and metal)

But I am more suspicious of Charles the Wise, the Noble, and the Well-Beloved (I make none of these up!)—and especially wary of the most common of all tags: the Great.

But if "the Great" ever legitimately applied to any ruler, I would surely pick Peter (1672–1725), even over Charlemagne himself. Peter lived his life as on the set of *Cats,* with every item scaled up way above normal size. At 6 feet 7 inches, he towered over his contemporaries; and his demonic, obsessive, unrelenting energy surpassed the common store, even more than his physical size exceeded normal bounds. If anyone ever deserved the cliché "larger than life," picture Peter the Great in the midst of his gartantuan carouses, his terrifying cruelties, his incessant wars, his obsessive need to learn and experience, his overwhelming drive to modernize and to make efficient.

Peter could not live vicariously. If modernization and success in war required a navy (to win access to the Baltic Sea by defeating Sweden and to challenge Turkey's control of the Black Sea), then Peter had to design his own ships, and therefore had to learn carpentry, ironworking, and shipbuilding. When he initiated and joined the "Great Embassy" in 1697–1698, a

2. Eye made of glass, antler bone, and metal

delegation of more than 150 sent to learn European ways and trades, Peter spent months working incognito at shipyards in Holland and England. (He dressed in worker's clothes and took humble lodgings, but his height always betrayed him, and people came to gawk.) He boasted proficiency in fifteen trades, including masonry, carpentry, printing, cobbling, and dentistry—though he took greatest pride in turning objects on his lathe, and in metalwork.

Did ever a more complex or enigmatic man rule a great nation at so crucial a time (made so largely by his own personality). Peter was brilliant, but scarcely contemplative. He would thrust himself (and thus his nation) into action impetuously and on a grand scale. Sometimes he withdrew in defeat and frustration, but often he enjoyed great success. His forced industrialization (largely for construction of war materiel) and his eventual defeat of Sweden after more than twenty years of nearly continuous war brought Russia into modernity, but at a fearsome price. His taxations were onerous and his services crushing—in manufactories, on battlefields, and in building St. Petersburg at the loss of tens of thousands of lives, largely to malaria and with no apparent indication of abiding concern on Peter's part. At his death, the serfs of Russia were even more oppressed and more tightly bound to their lords and lands than ever before.

3. Bark books

Peter murdered and maimed his declared enemies by the thousands. He would break a dishonest tax collector on the wheel (not a figurative statement, but a literal description of an old instrument of torture, still current in Peter's Russia), and kill rebellious serfs and soldiers with the knout (a particularly nasty form of whip). He put his own son to death, though not without provocation and great heaviness of heart. According to legend, he once presented his wife with the head of her lover. (The legend goes on to relate her apparent unconcern and the eventual disposition of the head in Peter's collection, soon to be discussed. Catherine the Great, to finish the tale, finally ordered a proper burial for the head.)

On the other hand, he could be fierce in loyalty, prescient in vision, and compassionate in practice. Consider only the manner of his death. In November 1724, when sailing to visit an ironmongery, he saw another boat run aground, and immediately leapt into the icy water to rescue the commoners aboard. He never overcame the resulting fever and died three months later.

But among the admirable traits of this exceedingly mercurial and complex man, none surpasses, his thirst, his true passion, for knowledge, primarily of science and the practical arts. Here the great tsar became humble, and took as his motto: "For I am one of those who are taught and I seek those who will teach me." And he accepted instruction—from the numerous memoranda of his confidant, the preeminent philosopher Leibniz, to the practical advice of the humblest shipwright at Amsterdam or Deptford. He tried to return the fruits of his learning—by establishing schools, by promoting the printing of books (with a simplified font of his own invention), even by opening his collection to public view as a museum in 1714 with the motto: "I want people to look and learn."

As part of his liberality in learning, and as a manifestation of his intellectual zeal and restlessness, Peter the Great established one of his century's finest collections in natural history. He followed (and tried to outdo) a practice traditional in his own time, but quite foreign to our own. The tastes of his grand and mannered age spilled forth in many directions (art, architecture, and music, for example, all have distinctive styles touted in generations of scholarly monographs, European tour guides, and record jackets as "baroque"). Natural history collections caught the spirit of the age as well, particularly in a mode of accumulation and display aptly named the *Wunderkammer*, or cabinet of wonders. Collectors vied for the biggest, the most beautiful, the weirdest, and the most unusual. To stun, more than to order or to systematize, became the watchword of this enterprise. Objects of all sorts, sizes, and provenances could be mixed together—stuffed animals with ethnographic curios, bones with gold coins. The exotic and the old; a delight for the eyes and a challenge to the mind. Peter, following this tradition, called his collection a *Kunstkammer*, or chamber of curiosities. His collection forms the basis of the Leningrad museum to this day; Rosamond Purcell's glasnost-inspired visit pays homage to Peter's vision across the centuries.

In deciding what and how to collect, Peter sought the world's best advice of Leibniz, who wrote a fascinating memo in 1708, emphasizing the joy and pleasure of objects in great range and scope:

> Such a cabinet should contain all significant things and rarities created by nature and man. Particularly needed are stones, metals, minerals, wild plants, and their artificial copies [that is, products of human cultivation], animals both stuffed and preserved....Foreign works to be acquired should include diverse books, instruments, curiosities and rarities....In short, all that could enlighten and please the eye.

But Leibniz also touted the responsibilities of integration and education: "It is absolutely essential that they should be such as to serve not only as objects of general curiosity, but also as a means to the perfection of the arts and sciences."

Peter, who did nothing by half, sent lieutenants throughout his empire and beyond, both to collect and to study the *Wunderkammern* of other—for Peter followed his own motto in seeking instruction from experts. In 1711, for example, he dispatched his librarian, J. Schumacher, "to visit the museums of learned men, both public and private, and there to observe how Your Majesty's museum differs from theirs; and if there is anything lacking in

Your Majesty's museum to strive to fill the gap." Schumacher returned with much advice and a treasure trove of objects, including ancient Roman lamps, and engraved shells from Utrecht.

Peter's *Kunstkammer* contained many ingredients of the traditional "wonder chamber,"

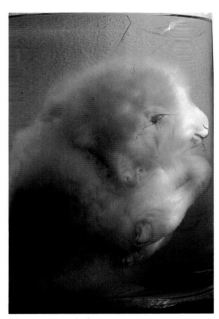

4. Two-headed sheep

including such oddities of nature as a four-legged rooster (photo 5) and a two-headed sheep (photo 4). But Peter put his personal stamp upon his collection by including many objects of his favored trades (the surgical instruments of photo 17, and his own portrait hammered in metal, (photo 7), his manufactories (the metal bar of photo 6, inscribed "Peter made this"), and his affairs of state (his globe in photo 8, turned to his spheres of war; a packet of his own hair, so labeled and used to make his wig, juxtaposed with a death mask of his most determined but respected enemy, Charles XII of Sweden, in photo 10). Consider, especially, the slightly humorous, slightly gruesome display of human teeth in photo 9, all personally pulled by Peter, who fancied himself a dentist, and who would often demand this sacrifice of a member of his retinue, or even of an idle passerby. The exhibit inspired the followed entry in the Leningrad catalogue: "teeth extracted by Emperor Peter from various persons," including "a singer" (number 6), "a person who made tablecloths" (number 10), "a bishop of Rostov" (number 23), "Madame Re who was named the Emperor's nurse" (number 25), and "a fast-walking messenger" (but not fast enough—number 45). I can only sympathize with the victim and recall one of the Mikado's tortures to "make the punishment fit the crime"

> *His teeth, I've enacted,*
> *Shall all be extracted*
> *By terrified amateurs.*

Several contemporary descriptions permit a reconstruction of Peter's collection as it appeared on public display. Five rooms contained the basic collection of natural and ethnographic objects—anatomical preparations of organs, embryos, and oddities preserved in alcohol and displayed in glass jars, stuffed birds, dried fish, a mounted elephant, and large quantities of ivory. (When Peter died in 1725, his curator estimated that undisplayed material might fill another twenty-five to thirty rooms.) One gallery contained portraits, statues, reliefs, and actual skeletons, including (after his death in 1724), the bones of the giant

5. Four-legged rooster

Bourgeois, Peter's personal footman, acquired during his foreign travels and standing more than 7 feet tall. Another gallery, dubbed "the Emperor's workshop," contained Peter's lathes and displayed his "works of the chisel" and "turned works." Still another featured *Kunststücke*, or works of virtuosity, including sets of spheres within spheres made of ivory and wood, and a graded series of 100 beakers, fitting one into the other ("like a set of Russian dolls," to cite the conventional simile, but more appropriately than usual in this case). Peter even included live exhibits of deformed and unusual people, including a hermaphrodite (who escaped despite his/her[1] stipend of twenty rubles per year), and the celebrated Foma, who had only two digits on each hand and foot and who walked and collected money for public amusement. When Foma died, he was stuffed and exhibited next to Bourgeois.

Peter built his collection bit by bit; yet, as Catherine would later furnish the Hermitage by mass purchase, Peter also bought some great *Wunderkammern* intact—and these served as the foundation (and distinction) of his total effort. When Peter visited Holland in 1697, he took time out from his apprenticeship in naval architecture to meet the finest scientists of this most enlightened land. He discussed anatomy and physiology with the great Boerhaave in Leiden, and he marveled at the hidden worlds in Leeuwenhoek's microscopes in Delft. Above all, he enjoyed the company, attended university lectures, and reveled in the magnificent collection

6. Metal bar "Made this" (Peter)

of Frederick Ruysch, described by a recent biographer as "probably the most skilled and knowledgeable preparator in the history of anatomy." Peter found one embalmed child so touching and realistic that he bent down and kissed the infant's face.

When Peter returned to Holland in 1717, he sought out Ruysch and greeted him with the words: "you are still my same old teacher." Peter bought Ruysch's entire stock of some 2,000 anatomical preparations for the grand sum of 30,000 Dutch guilders. On the same trip, Peter purchased the largely ethnographic *Wunderkammer* of the apothecary Albert Seba. These two great Dutch collections—but particularly Ruysch's for natural history—became the centerpiece and chief glory of Peter the Great's *Kunstkammer*. Indeed, nearly three centuries later, Rosamond Purcell's own path to

---

[1] I abominate this solution to the linguistic problems of sexism—but what a pleasure to use it properly in this case!

Russia and to the remnant of Peter's collection lay in following Ruysch's trail from Leiden to Leningrad.

Peter the Great and Frederik Ruysch may strike us, at first, as the ultimate odd couple in profession and temperament, but the links are as tight and as complex as the vascular trees of Ruysch's finest preparations. Frederik Ruysch (1638–1731), who enjoyed more than ninety-three years of life in an age usually marked by early death, taught anatomy to students and midwives at the Amsterdam Surgeon's Guild for more than fifty years. As a young student, with medical degree just in hand, Ruysch published an important treatise on his discovery of

7. Portrait of Peter the Great hammered in metal (c. 1½ x 2 ft.)

8. Small brass globe

valves in the lymphatic system. But his heart and skill lay more in preparation and embalming than in research and publication.

In this great age of medical anatomy, Ruysch developed special and unparalleled virtuosity in the crucial technique of revealing the courses of blood and other vessels by injecting substances into organs. The great embalmers and preparators kept their ingredients secret, but Ruysch apparently used some combination of wax, resin, talcum, and cinnabar pigment. The injected fluid had to perfuse all the vessels without rupturing them, and then harden only after filling the complete system—a set of stringent requirements indeed. (In fact, Ruysch never found a substance that could perfuse and harden in the tiny capillaries as well as the larger vessels. His most famous student, B. S. Albinus (1697–1770), the only man who ever exceeded his skills in preparation, later developed a technique to visualize capillaries as well.)

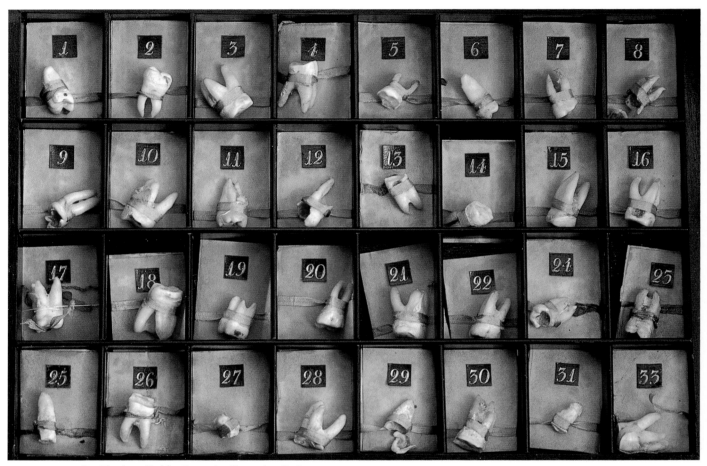

9. Teeth pulled by Peter the Great (see list)

10. Death mask of Charles XII, packet of hair from Peter the Great

Ruysch, the ultimate perfectionist's perfectionist and professional's professional, labored on his collection for nearly three quarters of a century. His appointment as Doctor to the Court in 1679 provided him with ample material for his preparations—for he now had access to dead babies found in the harbor and to the bodies of executed criminals. Ruysch worked on and on, enlisting his entire family in his preparations. He made exquisite and elegant displays of material that many people might regard today as gruesome—entire fetuses and neonates, body parts, organs with their vascular systems beautifully injected— all preserved in alcohol and placed in glass jars. He augmented this central focus upon anatomical preparation and embalming with the accoutrements of any good *Wunderkammer*— dried or stuffed fishes, plants, birds, and butterflies, the more exotic the better; ethnographic curios; and medical peculiarities of all kinds, from siamese twins to skeletal deformities. Among his oddities, for example, Ruysch displayed a box of fly eggs taken from the anus of a "distinguished gentleman who sat too long in the privy" (Ruysch's own description from his catalogue). When Peter the Great bought this entire collection and transported it, *virgo intacta*, to his *Kunstkammer* in St. Petersburg, he achieved one of the great coups in the history of collecting and brought the elegance and sophistication of old Europe into the heart of his new capital. As emblems of Russia's modernization, Ruysch's bones and bottles of organs rank as high as Peter's ships and his newly beardless boyars.

11. Arm holding eye socket, Collection Albinus, Leiden

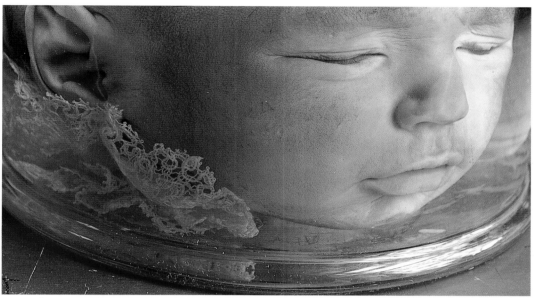

12. Baby with pink face, Ruysch

Peter's attraction to Ruysch transcended the objects that he wished to purchase, for these two men, so apparently different as impetuous tsar and meticulous embalmer, were surely soulmates in larger matters of spirit. Both possessed that rare temperament of most great achievers — tireless and obsessive commitment to a chosen species of excellence, whatever its content. No eighteenth century equivalent of goofing off in the afternoon and taking in a round of golf! In 1722, at age eighty-four, Ruysch wrote to Boerhaave: "Never does the sun rise too early for me, and nightfall always comes sooner than I would wish" (also an interesting comment on the limitations of artificial light before Edison).

But their main concordance lay in a common fascination for extremes and limits of human form, experience, and behavior — in a willingness to act and explore in realms that most people would shun as macabre or gruesome. For the restless and powerful Peter, this drive often ended in cruelty and the baroque extravagances of court. For the consummate craftsman Ruysch, this urge took palpable form in meticulous and idiosyncratic preparations within glass jars. For both men, the need to explore and capture the bizarre found ideal expression in the tradition of collecting then current — the *Wunderkammer*, with its emphasis on the exotic, and its keen understanding that fascination often arises from fear.

Many people today, in the midst of an age that prides itself on maximal tolerance and sophistication, are repelled, even sickened, by Ruysch's presentations. He might sever the arm of a dead child, surround it "so prettily and naturally" (his own words) with a sleeve and lace cuff expertly sewn by his young daughter Rachel, and then suspend from the fingers, by

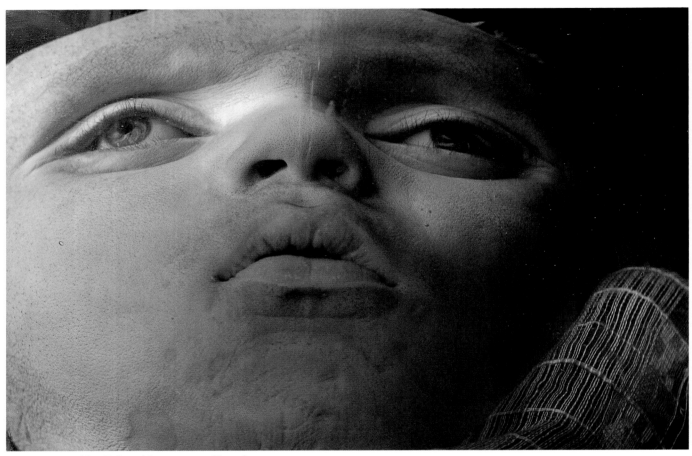

13. Baby with open eyes, Ruysch

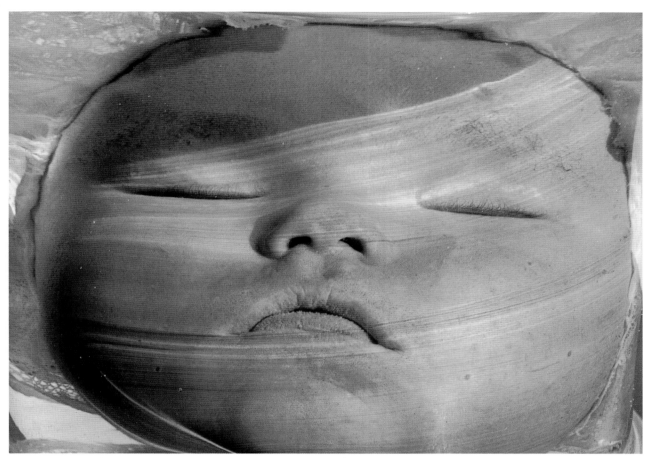

14. Baby with closed eyes, Ruysch specimen, Leiden

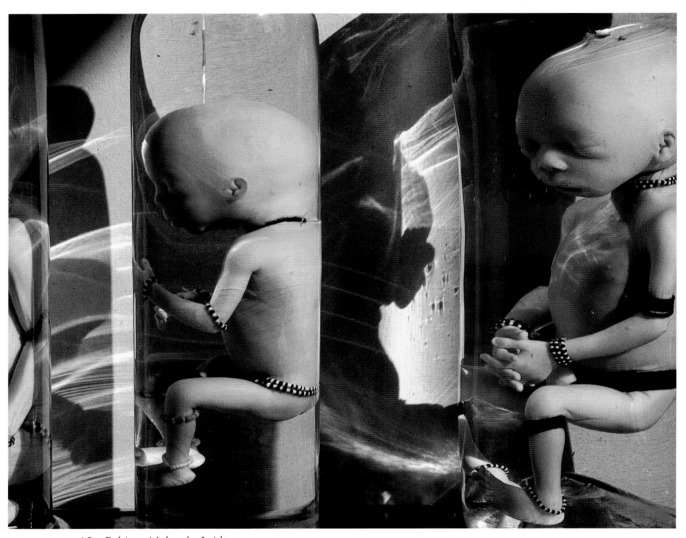

15. Babies with beads, Leiden

16. Baby with beads, Leningrad

an organic thread made of yet another body part, some exquisitely preserved and injected organ—perhaps an eye, or a bit of genital anatomy (see photo 11 for a similar preparation by his student Albinus). Or he might decapitate a fetus, preserve the face with elegant detail and lifelike pose, expose the brain, and then place this artifact of death into a glass jar (see photos 13 & 14). (My very words will inspire a gag reaction in some modern readers, even without the accompanying photographs. We fought hard with our editors for the privilege of including these difficult objects in our book. They represent an alien aesthetic that we must try to understand, and they probe our own humanity by bringing us to the limits of Terence's famous maxim: *Homo sum: humani nil a me alienum puto*—I am a man, and nothing human is alien to me.)

To understand Ruysch (and Peter) with proper empathy, we must grasp two features of seventeenth-century life that are maximally different from our own sensibilities. First, we have banished death from public view as a condition of age best experienced in hospitals and other sequestered places. In Ruysch's time, death was a persistent and omnipresent (if unwelcome) guest, a companion of all ages and classes. People lived face to face with corruption and disfiguration. If you cannot distance yourself from such a burden, why not make it an object of art, a species of elegance encased in glass?

17. Surgical tools belonging to Peter

Secondly, how can a post-modern and minimalist age understand the extensive and obsessive ornaments, the emotional exaggerations, both visual and spiritual, of baroque style? I stare at the ceiling of Melk Abbey in disbelief. I do not know what to make of *La Transparente* in the Cathedral of Toledo—a brilliantly white statue of Jesus (carved in 1730 by a man with the appropriate name of Narciso Tome), shown diving through a hole in the roof, feet in the air, arms extended, and surrounded by cherubs. I do not pretend to understand the aesthetic of Frederik Ruysch, who could turn death to elegance and use dismembered bits of the human body, exquisitely injected to reveal all the complexities of vascular circulation, as ornaments of larger compositions. Ruysch was the consummate baroque artist of the most intimate and familiar theme of death. I may not empathize, but I do accept, and I must struggle to comprehend.

Organs suspended from severed hands are challenging enough, but we began our work on this chapter in an unsuccessful search for the most bizarre of all Ruysch's productions. Ruysch made about a dozen *tableaux*, constructed of human fetal skeletons with backgrounds of other body parts, on allegorical themes of death and the transiency of life. (He also made simpler constructions on more obvious moral themes—the skull of a prostitute kicked by the leg of a baby, for example.) Ruysch built the "geological" landscapes of these *tableaux* from gallstones and kidneystones, and "botanical" backgrounds from injected and hardened major veins and arteries for "trees," and more ramified tissue of lungs and smaller vessels for "bushes" and "grass." The fetal skeletons, several per *tableau*, were ornamented with symbols of death and short life—hands may hold mayflies (which live but a day in their adult state); skulls bemoan their fate by weeping into "handkerchiefs" made of elegantly injected mesentery or brain meninges; "snakes" and "worms," symbols of corruption made of intestine, wind around pelvis and rib cage. Quotations and moral exhortations, emphasizing the brevity of life and the vanity of earthly riches, festooned the compositions. One fetal skeleton holding a string of pearls in its hand proclaims, "Why should I long for the things of this world?" Another, playing a violin with a bow made of a dried artery, sings, "Ah fate, ah bitter fate."

Unfortunately, these exquisitely delicate displays have apparently not survived the rigors of time—the fires, moves, wars, winters, and changes of government (while organs in alcohol protected by glass jars fared better). But Rosamond made another discovery about the Ruyschiana of Leningrad. When Ruysch died in 1731, his widow auctioned off the remaining items of his collection. Few distinguished works remained, for Peter had carried off the bulk of a lifetime's work. The years since have taken their further toll, and few of Ruysch's preparations can now be found in his native Holland. In particular, the Leiden Museum, in Ruysch's own center of operation, laments its poor representation of such a distinguished native son. The museum holds several unlabeled preparations that seem to have the elegance and macabre character of Ruysch's work, but have not been properly identified and have therefore been attributed to later collectors. Included here are fetuses in jars, festooned with beads (photo 15). Rosamond found others of identical style and ornamentation in the midst of Ruysch's material in Leningrad (photo 16)—and the favored, but unexpected, identification with Ruysch (for the Leiden specimens) now seems firm. The signature of the master extends across nations and centuries. You lose most battles in the drive to retain and restore information, for time is a better eraser than embalmer; but you win some.

Catherine the Great did not share her grandfather-in-law's love for collections in the old baroque style of accumulated oddities. She lived in the new age of enlightenment order, the encyclopedists and system builders. She viewed Peter's "universal" type of museum as an anachronism, and bemoaned the vanity of even thinking that nature might be so enclosed. She wrote of a curator who still favored Peter's style: "I often quarreled with him about his wish to enclose Nature in a cabinet—even a huge palace could not hold Her." So Ruysch's own mottoes, emblazoned in his *tableaux*, soon applied to his own compositions in Russia as well as to life itself. *Vita quid est? Fumus fugiens et bulla caduca* (What is life? A transient smoke and a fragile bubble). *Volat irrevocabile tempus* (Time flies and cannot be recalled). But we still marvel at the power of ancient artifacts to disturb, and to instruct.

Note about Peter's Hair #10; collection #1508: hairs from his wig which were made of his own hair, c. 1729. His own hair cut because of extreme heat.

NOTE: Specimens come either from the Kunstkammer of Peter the Great at the Leningrad branch of the N. N. Miklukho-Maklay Institute of Ethnography, USSR Academy of Sciences, or from the Museum of Anatomy and Embryology of the State University of Leiden in the Netherlands.

2 A GENTLEMAN IN JAPAN

When I studied high school American history in the heroic mode, we were taught that Commodore Matthew C. Perry sailed his four "black ships" into Tokyo Bay in 1853, thus forcing trade with the West and initiating a series of events that would topple the Tokugawa shogunate and lead to the Meiji restoration (and the beginning of a military modernization that would eventually recoil upon us at Pearl Harbor). Perry, in this interpretation, was the apostle of an inexorable and inevitable march to technological progress and integration among nations. The avowedly isolationist policy of pre-Perry Japan had forced a rapid transition instead of the usual steady pace — but the beat of history went on.

The fallacies of this interpretation are legion, beginning with the hyperpatriotic and more than faintly racist assumptions involved in viewing Perry as bringing the gift of modernity. But the very premise of the argument — that Japan had stagnated in perpetual isolation before — is factually false. Japan had not always shut its doors to Western trade and influence; the two centuries of closure, ended by events that Perry helped to unleash, represented a conscious policy of reversal.

Portuguese ships first reached Japan in the mid-sixteenth century, bringing those twin tools of disruption from the Western juggernaut: muskets and missionaries. Many of the *daimyos* (feudal lords) welcomed the opportunity for enrichment and power that foreign trade represented. Since Western traders often demanded a *quid pro quo* in landing missionaries with trade goods, Christianity began to flourish as well. Francis Xavier himself arrived on a Jesuit mission in 1549 and spent more than two years in Japan.

In winning the battle of Sekigahara in 1600, the powerful *daimyo* Tokugawa Ieyasu established national supremacy and, three years later, legalized his position by establishing the Tokugawa shogunate at Edo (the old name for Tokyo). Ieyasu favored foreign trade (under restrictions) and expanded the sources from Catholic Portugal to Protestant England and Holland as well. After Ieyasu died in 1616, his successors slowly established the policy of *sokaku*, or national seclusion. The later shoguns began to view foreign influence as a threat to their hegemony for two major reasons: (1) trade fueled the power of local *daimyos* and raised the specter of renewed fragmentation; (2) the continued spread of Christianity weakened central state rule. Ieyasu had begun to restrict Christianity, but his successors moved towards total suppression, even at the cost of foreign trade. In 1637, farmers led by masterless Christian samurai rebelled at Kyushu and held out for five months until all 30,000 were slaughtered by the Shogun's forces.

At this point, the shogunate did impose strict closure and began what one historian has called "the strangest experiment in world history; a great, highly developed country closed itself to the rest of the world." So complete and sudden was the cutoff that Japanese

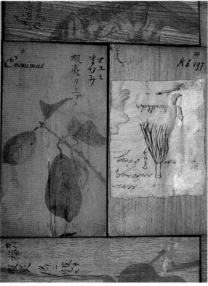

18. Tree leaves painted on corresponding woods

19. Pressed Japanese rose

inhabitants of various trading cities established abroad (mostly in other oriental nations) were not even allowed to return home. All Western trade was reduced to the merest trickle. Only Holland could send ships, and only two per year. These ships could only land at Nagasaki, and all Dutch traders had to live on the artificial island of Dejima, connected to the rest of Nagasaki by a narrow and easily-watched causeway.

One can hardly imagine a situation less conducive to establishing collections in natural history. Western science knew virtually nothing about the indigenous fauna and flora of Japan. In these limited circumstances, Philip Franz von Siebold (1796–1866) gently exposed

20. *Union nodularia japanensis*

the world of Japanese zoology as surely as Perry and others would open (so much more dubiously) the doors of trade.

Von Siebold, a German from Würzburg, chose to slake his *Wanderlust* by working as a physician in the Dutch East Indies (where the prospect of pursuing his interest in natural history served as an important and not so subsidiary motive). Von Siebold arrived at Batavia (now Djakarta) in February, 1823. He made such a favorable impression on the colonial powers that they offered him the post, then open, of physician at Dejima—for tradition dictated that this position be filled by a man who could also study and collect in various branches of natural history (might as well choose a polymath if only one person can go).

Von Siebold arrived in Japan on August 12, 1823, and remained until the end of 1829. At first, he was restricted to Dejima with the rest of the small European community. But he was eventually permitted to visit patients in Nagasaki and to collect medicinal herbs in and around town. Von Siebold's reputation as a fine physician spread and, in 1824, he was allowed to purchase a plot of land in Nagasaki itself, where he built a hospital and school (for his lectures, in Dutch, on natural history and medicine).

Von Siebold became more and more immersed in Japanese life. He found what our generation calls a "significant other" in a woman named Sonogi, and had a daughter who later became one of the first women physicians in Japan. He built a botanical garden at Dejima and

21. Hermit crabs

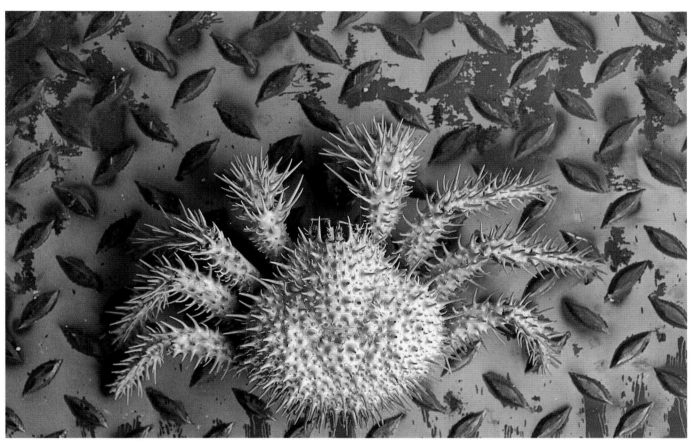

22. Coconut crab

23. Japanese raccoon dogs

A Gentleman in Japan

24. Head of a macaque

cultivated more than a thousand Japanese plants (see photo 18). His medical patients were not allowed to pay cash for his services, but, von Siebold took recompense in kind by accepting gifts of objects in ethnography and natural history.

After working for three years from his limited outpost at Dejima (and depending upon gifts from Japanese friends and patients for material from other parts of the country), von Siebold got his big break in 1826, as another consequence of the same history that had originally closed Japan to foreign influence. As part of their strategy to limit the power of the *daimyos*, the Tokugawa shoguns required feudal lords to make annual or biennial visits to the court at Edo, and to keep part of their family (as virtual hostages) in this seat of temporal power. The chief of the Dutch establishment at Dejima made the traditional visit to Edo as well—if more as a voluntary act of diplomacy than a requirement of fealty. At first, in the seventeenth century, the Dutch chiefs travelled annually, but the visits had been reduced to once in four years by von Siebold's time. Since the Japanese maintained a strong interest in Western medicine, the physician of the trading post usually joined the visit to Edo.

Thus, in 1826, von Siebold finally obtained his one chance to traverse virtually the entire length of Japan. Von Siebold's own movements were limited (tradition dictated, for example, that he be carried in a sedan chair along the route), but he was able to make some personal collections, and he obtained other material by purchase and by directing the less restricted Japanese members of the delegation. His fine collection from this trip included two Japanese wolves, two ibises, cranes, a living giant salamander (see photo 25), and several giant spider crabs.

Von Siebold's fortunes reached their apogee on this 1826 trip, but declined rapidly thereafter. His boldness and unwillingness to follow all diplomatic restrictions (prompted mainly by his zeal in acquiring specimens for his collection) caused an irreparable rift with the chief of the trading post. The appointment of a new chief (for other reasons) delayed von Siebold's termination for a while, but he was ordered back to Batavia in 1828. With his collections already en route to Leiden, and following the destruction of his botanical garden by a typhoon, the worst storm hit on December 16, 1828.

This incident, usually called the "Siebold affair" in historical writing, has never been properly elucidated, and still excites passions (a popular Japanese novel, written in the late 1970s, centered upon this episode and strongly suggested that von Siebold had long been a spy for the Dutch government—though von Siebold's general reputation remains high in Japan). Von Siebold had corresponded with the court astronomer Takahashi. In exchange for books and instruments, Takahashi sent maps of the Japanese empire to von Siebold—an illegal and even treasonous act under Tokugawa rules of national seclusion. Von Siebold, warned of impending troubles, copied the maps and successfully hid his facsimiles. Takahashi was arrested and von Siebold's house and other buildings in Dejima were searched by the police. Von Siebold was not allowed to leave Japan and was often, and severely, interrogated. He took all the blame upon himself and refused to mention names or to implicate any Japanese friends. Instead he offered himself as hostage, and eventually won

25. Print of salamander from "Fauna Japonica"

much admiration for his personal courage. In the final sentence, pronounced on October 22, 1829, von Siebold was permanently exiled from Japan (not too severe a punishment, since he had planned to leave anyway). Most Japanese suspects in the case were eventually freed, but Takahashi died in jail.

26.   Drawing of head of female Japanese macaque

Von Siebold apparently harbored no deep grudges, for he spent the rest of his life promoting interest in Japan and things Japanese. (He also made another two-year trip to Japan in 1859–1861, after Perry's forced visit had lifted the old restrictions.) As the most prominent of these efforts, von Siebold organized the work of several fine taxonomists and anatomists at Leiden (C. J. Temminck and H. Schlegel for vertebrates and W. De Haan for invertebrates) to produce a lavishly illustrated five-volume monograph entitled *Fauna Japonica*, based upon the material that he had collected during his first visit. Von Siebold's specimens remain in Leiden, where Rosamond took the photographs for this chapter. The *Fauna Japonica* includes four volumes on vertebrates (mammals, fishes, birds, and reptiles)—see photo 25— including a comparison of von Siebold's specimens with plates from the monograph.

Von Siebold worked in Japan under the most severe restrictions ever imposed upon a great collector in such a literate nation. He broke the isolation of Japan's fauna a generation before political power ruptured the seclusion of her people. I cannot imagine a more fitting tribute to this ecumenicism than the following image from modern Japanese history. The recently deceased emperor Hirohito was a noted expert in the taxonomy of marine invertebrates, and produced several competent works in invertebrate taxonomy. Since so many important Japanese species were first named in von Siebold's *Fauna Japonica*, we may be certain that Hirohito studied von Siebold's specimens as he pursued his own work. The Tokugawa shoguns had kept the emperor as a figurehead in Kyoto, while they exercised political power in Edo (Tokyo); they also kept the lid on von Siebold and his urge to collect throughout Japan. How fitting that both restrictions should be symbolically lifted by a modern emperor's study of the work that brought Japanese zoology to the rest of the world.

NOTE: The botanical and zoological specimens from the travels of von Siebold are held by the Nationaal Natuurhistorisch Museum in Leiden.

27. Macaque depicted in drawing

3 A TAXONOMIST'S TAXONOMIST

*I*n the never-ending struggle to distinguish fact from legend, look for "canonical stories" (constant lines, but shifting casts across centuries) as primary markers of myth. Ann Landers, a tough and discerning lady, was recently bamboozled by the following tale: A man wrote in, claiming that he had seen an ad for a Porsche, in excellent condition, selling for but $50. He assumed that the ad had mistakenly dropped two or three zeros before the decimal point, but went to see the car anyway. It was in beautiful shape, and $50 was the correct price. He purchased the car in disbelief and then, contract securely and irrevocably in hand (and quite unable to bear the pangs of curiosity), he inquired: "Why so cheap." She replied: "oh, my husband just ran off with his secretary. He asked me to sell all his stuff and send him the money." Ann believed it, but another man wrote in the next week: "I first heard the story fifty years ago, but it was a Packard for twenty bucks."

I have been fooled twice by such canonical legends. I once began a column with a famous story about Joseph Grimaldi, the first modern circus clown. A correspondent sent me the identical tale from an old Latin book about a Roman clown named Roscius. I began another column, again in good faith, with a story about a colleague who had recently died. This man was a great taxonomist of the old school—detailed, ordered, meticulous, and industrious to a fault. I was told that two boxes had been found in a desk drawer after his death—one marked "pieces of string for future use," the other marked "pieces of string not worth saving." Next year, to my chagrin, I received a book of "classical" New England humor. Its title—you guessed it—"Pieces of String Not Worth Saving."

This stereotype of zealous orderliness (and hyperfrugality) has often been applied, much to our detriment, to taxonomists and natural historians. We are said to be the fuddy-duddies and accountants of science—maintainers of the lists and guardians of the storehouses. The

28. Domestic dogs

haughty princes of more prestigious disciplines have often used this image to lord their status over us. The physicist Lord Rutherford, at the turn of the century, called us glorified stamp collectors. His equally exalted successor Luis Alvarez, angered that many dinosaur taxonomists had disputed his asteroidal impact theory of mass extinction, used the same image just three or four years ago: "I don't like to say bad things about paleontologists, but they're really not very good scientists. They're more like stamp collectors." (I happen to agree with Luis on the extinction issue, but I deplore his simile. I might also say that, as a former philatelist, I reject his disparagement from both sides.)

Three supposedly common elements fuel this persistent simile: (1) the need to "get 'em all," to fill all the spaces in the album, or check off all the bird species on your life list; (2) the obsession with measurement of trivial differences and the need to collect all versions (every variation in number of perforations—philatelists have "perforation gauges" for quick and accurate counting—or each nuance in number and shade of tail feathers or body scales; (3) order, order, order.

Stereotypes, clichés and canonical legends often arise from substrates of validity, whatever their simplistic exaggerations or unfair mockeries. Amidst the variety of natural historians, we do find a small genre of blitzkrieg collectors and hoarders who can turn a species or habitat into the equivalent of the martyred Vietnamese village described in the infamous words of an American military commander: "We had to destroy the town in order to save it." I study a West Indian land snail named *Cerion*. One of my predecessors, a manic collector who worked half a century ago, gathered *Cerion* by the tens of thousands (per site if available!). To this day, his specimens remain in large burlap bags, never opened or studied, in drawers of the Smithsonian Institution. I cannot for the life of me fathom what he thought he might ever do with so many shells. The science of statistics is dedicated to the proposition that you really don't have to get them all.

In the true spirit of natural history—the cherishing of honorable diversity (both in objects and doers)—we present this chapter on a fine collector who probably does come as close to the stereotype of "string not worth saving" as any taxonomist of note. Yet just as I once loved the triangular stamps of Tannu Tuva, ogled the reproduction of Goya's naked *maja* on a Spanish issue, admired the colors of San Marino's offerings to philatelists of the world (surely they were not meant for postage from this tiny principality), and tried to fill every Ceylonese space in my album—so too may we respect and appreciate the life and work of Willem Cornelis van Heurn (1887–1972).

Van Heurn's name will never loom large in the annals of science, for he spun no theories, invented no concepts, and coined no words. Among his hundred or so publications, the only item that even comes close to commenting on a conceptual issue in evolutionary theory appeared in 1955, under the charmingly anthropocentric title: "Do tits lay eggs together as the result of a housing shortage?" As I scan his list of writings, I note (in abundance) all the staples of the stereotype—the endless descriptions and odd observations of a gentle, harmless, diligent naturalist, ever out for a new tidbit, a previously unnoticed grain of sand on nature's beach. "Poaching in the service of ornithology" in 1921. "A Gecko with a forked tail" and "Cannibalism in frogs" in 1928. "Mortality of chicken broods during a thunderstorm" in 1957. "Wrinkled eggs" in 1958. "Extra premolars in the lower jaw of the mole" in 1959. "Our cat washes herself" in 1962. Consider the totality of van Heurn's output for 1927: "Some comments on the bats of Buitenzorg," "The rat question," "Shark and ray leather," "The safety instinct in chickens," "An observation of a cuckoo which, without evidence, would have been falsely interpreted," and, finally, the ultimate exhortation of the careful collector, "Good labelling."

Van Heurn, endowed with advantages of high birth and family wealth, studied biology at the University of Leiden and remained an associate and benefactor of the Natural History Museum, one of the world's oldest and best, throughout his life. The memorial booklet by L. B. Holthuis and A. M. Husson, published by the Museum after van Heurn's death, suc-cinctly stated his qualifications for his genre of science: "He made natural history collections wherever he went and gave his attention to almost all animal groups. He was an excellent shot, and a competent preparator; his mammal and bird skins are exemplary."

Taking full advantage of the limited Dutch empire, van Heurn went to Surinam in 1911, to Simaloer (an island off the west coast of Sumatra) in 1913, and to Dutch New Guinea in 1920–21. He then lived in the Dutch East Indies (mostly on Java) for fifteen years before returning to Holland in 1939. While in the Indies, he ran a laboratory for sea research, studied rat control on Java, Timor, and Flores, taught high school, and eventually became head of the botany department at the Netherlands Indies Medical School in Java. Everywhere he lived and travelled, van Heurn collected large series of specimens. These he would prepare and label in his particularly meticulous way. Most of this material ended up in the Leiden museum, where van Heurn himself worked as assistant curator for fossil mammals from 1941 to 1945, before moving to Wilp in the central Netherlands. Van Heurn continued his collecting at Wilp, concentrating (as ever) on local natural history — in this case, the moles underground and domestic animals in plainer sight.

Rosamond Purcell's photographs beautifully capture the spirit (both strength and foibles) of natural history in this style. Consider the sheer number gathered of the most ordinary creatures, with each skin lovingly prepared and arranged in identical form and posture — the dogs with their open mouths (photo 28), pigs with nose out and ears up (photo 32), above all, the plethora of moles, bodies flattened and forelegs splayed (photo 30). All prepared in exactly the same way, but collected to illustrate the differences among specimens that supply fuel to evolutionary change. (Van Heurn's two principal papers on moles treated variation in tooth number and coat color.) Do we not sense a paradox here, in such procedural sameness and rigid formality applied to nature's bounteous diversity? Consider, too, the focus on ordering and labeling, especially in the frugal mode of the taxonomist with boxes of string not worth saving. Note the flattened rodent skin housed in the envelope — the original recipient

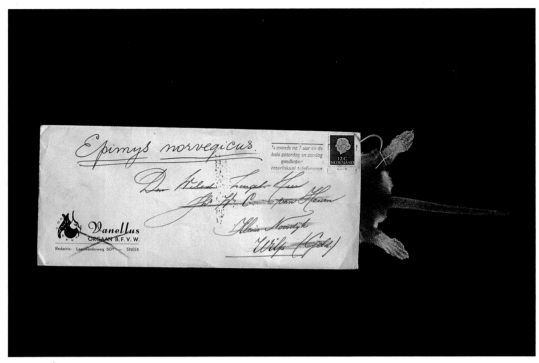

29. Rats in envelope

dutifully crossed off and the proper Latin for the rat inserted (photo 29). And the obsession with orderly measurement, whether or not any conceptual purpose be served. Photo 31 shows van Heurn's series of paper disks used to measure the curvature of pig's tusks.

But nature always wins in the end. You try, especially if a van Heurnian sense of tidiness be your temperament, to keep everything within proper categories and bounds (not to mention actual boxes). You even face nature's overt oddities with a drive to contain and classify (as in photo 33, showing van Heurn's collection of deformed eggs). But there is ultimately too much out there for one man, no matter how assiduous. Too much and too varied. Consider the "uncurated miscellany" of photo 34 — including fetal pigs, snakes, moles, mice, cat's guts, a "siamese twin" apple, slugs, frogs, and toads. (Photo 35 shows a detail of snake, mole, and double apple.)

Van Heurn represents an extreme in our eclectic and aesthetic survey of collecting styles — the hyperacquisitive finder and meticulous keeper. This style is easy enough to criticize, particularly from a modern perspective that offers both moral and theoretical doubt — the former from "animal rights" ethicists, the latter from evolutionists and statisticians who know that good samples yield better conclusions than misguided attempts to bag the entirety

30. European moles

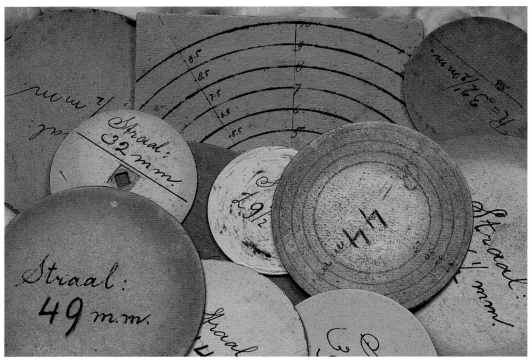

31. Paper discs used to measure curvature of pig tusks

(though the United States census, as constitutionally mandated, is still trying to count each person, nose by nose, every ten years).

But we will speak for van Heurn and his way, however outdated. He was, first of all, a paragon of commitment, dedication, and knowledge. His colleagues honored this industry and expertise by naming more than forty taxa in his honor over a period of as many years. These species and subspecies, all given the trivial name *heurni* or *vanheurni* (though he also became godfather to the reptilian genus *Heurnia*), span the full range of his concerns from mammals to mollusks (with a mite and several insects in between). Secondly, his legendary courtesy and kindness also betoken a gentler, if less intellectually robust, style of science that did not run entirely on grant proposals and egotism.

Nonetheless, I would base my major defense on an abstract principle, not on van Heurn's personal virtues. Nature's principal theme is infinite variety, both within the bounds of any species, and especially (and obviously) across the stunning range of form in any region or ecosystem. We, as primates evolutionarily committed to vision as a principal sense, comprehend this blooming and buzzing confusion by ordering and classifying, separating and comparing. Van Heurn's style represents a hypertrophy of this basic human instinct for

32. Domestic pigs

33. Selection of deformed eggs

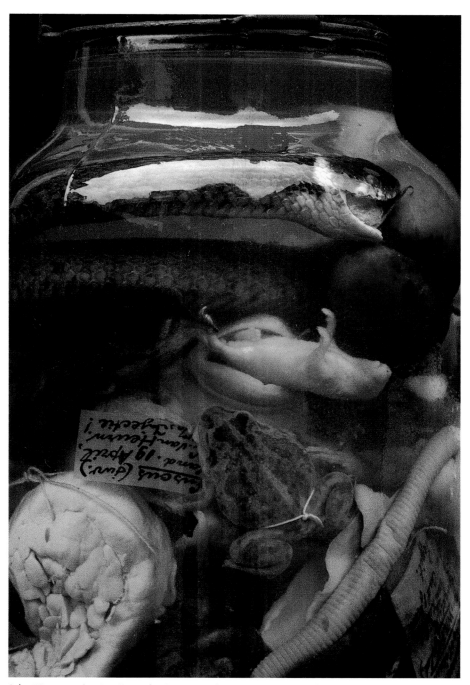

34. Uncurated miscellani: fetal pigs, snake, moles, mice, snake, double apple, cat's guts, slug, frog, toad

35. Detail of uncurated jar: snake, mole, double apple

A Taxonomist's Taxonomist

comprehension. Can anyone gainsay the undeniable beauty of his myriad of moles, each rigidly wrought in identical style (the categorization that grants us comprehension), but each just a little bit different (the variety that nature poses both to and against our quest for understanding).

If we value the diversity of natural objects, then we must also cherish the varieties of honorable human behavior. Van Heurn undoubtedly could have found an appropriate pigeon-hole for his own peculiarities. Picture him then in this little niche, as the objects of his lifelong passion look upon him, and intone Antony's final assessment of Brutus: "Nature might stand up and say to all the world, 'This was a man!'"

NOTE: The specimens of van Heurn are held by the Nationaal Natuurhistorisch Museum in Leiden.

4 MENTAL BOXING

*T*he fame and enduring reputation of Eugen Dubois rests entirely upon his discovery, in 1892, of the first fossil remains of a human ancestor—the so-called "Java Man" of older texts, now known as *Homo erectus* and regarded as the penultimate member of our lineage, the direct forebear of *Homo sapiens*. I doubt that one professional biologist in a hundred could identify Dubois for any other interest or achievement. Yet this chapter on Dubois contains no photography of these celebrated remains from Trinil—the skullcap and femur of the first *Homo erectus*. We omit this source of his fame because the Java bones played so small a role in his daily life and work during the heart of his career as a naturalist in the Netherlands. In fact, although Dubois worked intensely on the Java fossils during the 1890s, and took them out again for a new look and interpretation late in his life, the famous Trinil hominids remained in a locked vault—hidden from collegial doubters by the nearly paranoid Dubois—for nearly a quarter century. During this hiatus, Dubois pursued a long series of fascinating studies, intimately related to the Java fossils in intellectual focus, on the meaning and evolution of brain size in mammals. This work, which occupied far more of his career than the Java fossils and generated the bulk of his material legacy in museum collections, shall be our focus here.

As a prime quirk and oddity of history, many people become prisoners to their item of fame. They acquire an identification that can never again be shucked, no matter how fleeting the moment or how orthogonal to the rest of their lives. In an incident that lasted just a second or two, on October 10, 1920, Bill Wambsganss, Cleveland's second baseman, stabbed a line drive, doubled off the runner at second and tagged out another runner who had steamed in from first, thinking that the ball would surely go for a hit. Wamby (as the box scores called him) thus completed the only unassisted triple play in the history of the World Series. It was an odd play, but not a great effort—rather an automatic consequence of a highly unusual

36. Eye socket of fossil horse

circumstance. Yet Wambsganss, who had a long and far better than average career in baseball, is known for nothing else than his moment of unique fortuity. He is the sportsman's equivalent of the Latin writer who labored all his life, but produced only one item of note, and became *homo unius libri*, or the man of one book.

Homo erectus was no random moment in Dubois' career, but the apotheosis of a daring and well-conceived plan. Dubois reasoned that human ancestors might well be found in rocks of the right age and circumstance in Holland's East Asian possessions. He therefore enlisted as an army doctor, and had himself posted to Sumatra, and then to Java during the 1880s and early 1890s. There, following Pasteur's aphorism, fortune smiled upon Dubois' prepared mind, and he found the first hard evidence of our ancestry. He exhibited the fossils widely upon his return to Europe and provoked a great debate upon their interpretation. Although Dubois gained many supporters, and seemed to be winning the battle for acceptance of *Homo erectus* in his terms, he nonetheless reacted bitterly to his opponents and eventually, about 1900, locked the precious specimens up and kept them from sight for nearly a quarter century.

A canonical legend has arisen in paleontological circles to explain and exemplify Dubois' unusual behavior. The legend rests upon three claims: first, that Dubois withdrew his fossils because professional opinion had reviled and dismissed his interpretation; second, that Dubois then became a bitter and unproductive man, who never again produced any work of scientific merit; third, that when, late in life, Dubois again brought forth the Java fossils, his continuing dyspepsia led him to defeat, and he reinterpreted his former bright hope for human ancestry as nothing but a giant gibbon—a cruel joke and mockery of his original opinion.

Bert Theunissen's recent and excellent biography of Dubois, supplemented by the material evidence of this chapter, rebuts all three claims of the legend. On point one, we will surely not defend Dubois' incarceration of his fossils; his behavior was curious, idiosyncratic, and in violation of all professional standards. But, as Theunissen shows, Dubois was not proceeding from despair, in a rearguard action against his opponents. *Homo erectus* had provoked a major debate, but Dubois' opinion had fared well and seemed to be gaining ground when his paranoia vanquished his professionalism, and the slings and arrows of a waning minority provoked his rash action.

This reinterpretation of his withdrawal fits well with the debunking of the legend's second claim—his bitterness and subsequent nonproductivity. If he had locked up the fossils, said "to hell with all of you," and retired to his farm, all pieces of the canonical legend would have gelled. But Dubois did no such thing; he stayed at his post in Haarlem (as curator of the Teylers Museum and professor at the University of Amsterdam). There, beginning with an initial paper in 1898 (published in the midst of his first professional bout with *Homo erectus*), Dubois began an extensive and lifetime study—resulting in more than a score of fascinating publications and the development of a museum collection illustrated in this chapter—on a subject intimately and consciously linked with his work on the paleontology of human ancestry. Dubois, in short, moved his research in a collateral and expansive direction to study the evolution and functional meaning of brain size in mammals. He yearned to know the secrets of our large brain. How did humans evolve such an unparalleled mass of neural tissue, and what did it mean for our consciousness and intelligence? He had, as a first professional effort, tried to study the direct path of brain enlargement in our own lineage. Now, as a second attempt, he turned to the comparative assessment of brain size in all mammals, hoping to discover what makes humans so special within our genealogical group.

Dubois proceeded in a quantitative manner (however naively and, ultimately, incorrectly by modern standards). He first had to face a primary dilemma, long recognized and lamented (for example) by the likes of Georges Cuvier in the late eighteenth century. How can brains be compared in mammals of widely different body sizes (mice and elephants, or shrews and whales)? Disparity of size would pose no problem if mammals maintained a constant ratio of brain/body weight for brains of the same conceptual capacity. But such constancy does not hold: rather, brain weight increases more slowly than body weight as we move from small to large mammals of equivalent function and mental level. Consequently, a large mammal has an absolutely larger but a relatively smaller brain (by brain/body ratio) than an equivalent small mammal. Obviously, neither absolute brain weight, nor relative brain weight (brain/body ratio) can serve as a criterion—for whales would win by the first, and mice by the second, and both only by virtue of body size. Humans, who do deserve top billing despite our hubris, would win by neither false criterion: whales have absolutely larger brains, and shrews relatively larger brains, than ours.

The solution to this dilemma is now commonplace and undergirds a major activity in evolutionary biology—the study of *allometry*, or relative growth. Dubois (following an earlier lead by Otto Snell in 1891) was the initiator of these important studies in 1898—and his work on comparative brain size is far more extensive than his opinions on *Homo erectus*, though this larger side of Dubois' professional life has been forgotten on the Wambsganss principle of the tyranny of great moments.

Dubois reasoned that if the relationship of brain weight to body weight followed a regular course through the range of mammalian size, then a mathematical expression could be devised to determine the portion of brain size dependent upon the body mass. Using this expression, an "expected" brain weight could be calculated for a "standard" mammal at any body weight. The excess (or deficit) from this value, achieved by any actual organism, would be the measure of its superiority (or inferiority) in brain size relative to the mammalian standard. By this criterion, the superiority of the human brain would be measured by a maximal excess (or positive deviation from the standard curve) at our body weight.

Dubois' pioneering work on brain size has great value and deserves a rescue from two factors that decreed its oblivion—the Wambsganss effect that indissolubly links Dubois with a different effort, and Dubois' own pivotal errors in the quantification of brain size. Dubois made two key mistakes in his work on brain size. First, he miscalculated the rate of increase at $\frac{5}{9}$, arguing that brains grow $\frac{5}{9}$ as fast as bodies in moving from small to large mammals. Unfortunately, Dubois then took $\frac{5}{9}$ as an invariant mammalian standard, almost a law of nature—and he simply assumed this value (rather than checking by renewed calculations) in later papers. In fact, the actual average is closer to $\frac{2}{3}$, and by no means constant for all groups and all ranges of size. Second, Dubois deluded himself (and such a strong assessment must be made in the light of his dubious data) into thinking that values in excess of the standard clustered in groups differing by a factor of 2, or a doubling of brain size. He therefore developed an idiosyncratic, non-Darwinian theory of evolution by sudden doubling of brain size. In fact, the excess values for brainy species do not cluster into groups of even multiples (or into any clear groups at all); moreover, Dubois' cited values are wrong because he used the false $\frac{5}{9}$ value in removing the effects of body size.

Dubois amassed a museum collection, here illustrated in part, to support and further his work on brain size. Body weights must be taken from live animals (or, more dubiously, garnered from published values); they do not become parts of museum collections. But brain weights are measured by making casts of the skull cavity and then assessing their volumes. Dubois therefore built an extensive collection of brain casts for a large range of vertebrate species. We were intrigued by the humble paraphernalia of such important collections— the careful writing of Dubois' name directly upon a skull (photo 37); the neat lettering upon apothecary boxes used to house the smaller casts (we show a chicken and a bat on photo 38); above all by that stalwart mainstay of nineteenth- and early twentieth-century museum collections throughout the world—the cigar box with its recycled contents and packaging material (photo 40,

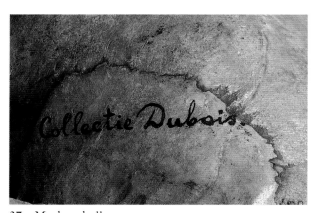

37. Monkey skull

39). Despite their current unpopularity in a more health-conscious world, their banning from restaurants and airplanes, their decline in acceptability and their relegation to dark-paneled rooms in superannuated men's clubs, all zoologists should pay professional homage to the cigar. Many of the most important specimens in the world are housed in cigar boxes.

If the housing and paraphernalia intrigued us, we were no less moved by the form of brain casts themselves. Their bilateral symmetry and complex grouping of paired bulbs, pouches, and excrescences almost inevitably suggests metaphorical comparison with the similarly symmetrical bodies of humans and other vertebrates (how fitting since Dubois collected these

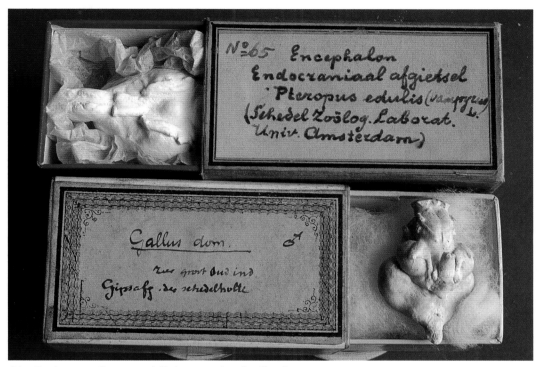

38. Brain casts of *pteropus edulls (vampyrus)* and *gallus dom*

data for comparison with body sizes). These appearances also recall Dubois' first career as anthropologist and give a kind of eerie consistency, in image and metaphor, to his two professional passions. One cigar box (photo 42) seems to hold a group of six human figurines; another suggests a set of decapitated torsos (photo 41); while a third shows all the concupiscence and symmetry of a true archaeological treasure—the Venus of Willendorf (photo 44).

The integration of part one (the Java fossils) and the larger part two (studies on mammalian brain size) of Dubois' career dispels the third part of the legend—*Homo erectus* bitterly defeated and reincarnated as a giant gibbon—and provides an intellectual union of his worlds akin to the metaphorical links we see in his cigar boxes. In the 1920s, Dubois finally unlocked the vaults and brought the Java fossils out for renewed study. The reasons for his change of heart are complex and include some unsubtle pressure from the Dutch parliament (inspired by complaints of scientists throughout the world). But Dubois had a positive reason as well, one rooted in the brain work of his second career, for Dubois thought that his rules of brain size had unlocked the true meaning of *Homo erectus*, and he therefore had to free the fossils in order to declare the good news.

39. Brain casts of squirrels

Remember that Dubois now held a saltatory view of evolution by sudden doubling of brain size. *Homo erectus*, to be a human ancestor under this scheme, should therefore show a cranial capacity of some 700 cc, or half that of modern humans. But the Trinil skullcap yielded·a figure closer to 1000 cc, and such braininess would eliminate *Homo erectus* from our immediate ancestry and relegate it to a terminal side branch under Dubois' theory. But Dubois wanted maximal status for his first scientific child: He wanted *Homo erectus* as a direct ancestor. He achieved his goal (wrongly we are now firmly convinced) by offering a new reconstruction for the body size of the Trinil hominid. If the Trinil femur belonged to a man of modern proportions, then *Homo erectus* weighed no more than 150 pounds—and its brain was too large (under Dubois' theory) for the penultimate stage of direct human ancestry. But, if the femur belonged to a creature with proportions more like those of a modern gibbon, then the body

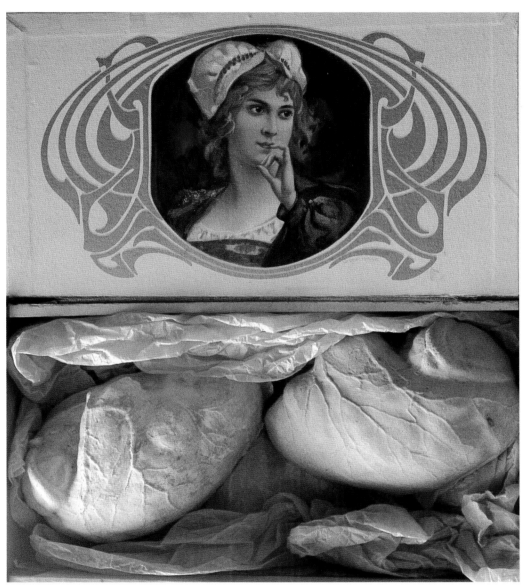

40. Brain cast of tiger

41. *Minimum Nicotine*

42. *Melati*

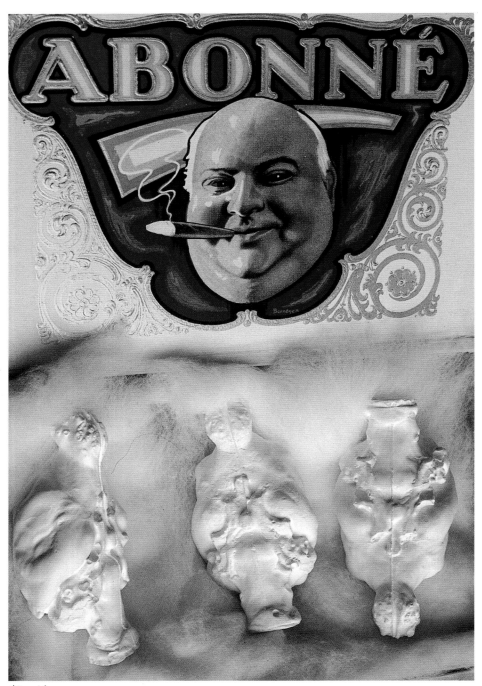

43. *Abonne*

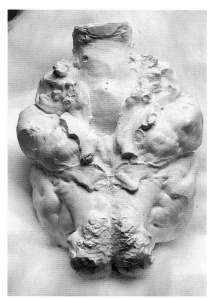

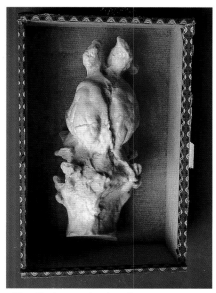

44. Brain cast of polar bear

45. Brain cast in cigar box

weight rose to greater than 220 pounds. Working back down the ⅝ curve, a 220 pound *Homo erectus* with a Trinl-sized brain would have, at the weight of a modern human, a brain exactly half our size! Thus Dubois reconstructed *Homo erectus* with the proportions of a giant gibbon in order to make it a true and direct human ancestor under his curious evolutionary theory. This argument, however fallacious in our eyes, was, for Dubois, an act of affimation, not of despair.

The world is messy; the world is multifarious. Nature is not the domain of the numerologist, not the realm for a seeker of Pythagorean absolutes. Brains do not evolve by clean doublings, producing a golden staircase to the stars, with pure smooth steps and no slop left over. Nature fills the spaces between Platonic absolutes—as we fill the drawers of our museums with all these wondrous details, with a richness and diversity more than adequate to replace geometrical dreams with the manifest and palpable beauty of objects.

NOTE: The Collection of Dubois is held by the Nationaal Natuurhistorisch Museum in Leiden.

5 THE VARIED FACETS OF PARADISE

I never know whether to look them up under "birds" (too broad) or "paradise" (a bit off the general subject) in indices of ornithology. They are the most baroque and beautiful creatures on earth, but their name is not a testimony to their exquisite appearance. They live only in the region of New Guinea, and were known to seafarers and oriental traders for centuries before any Westerner found their home. The natives of New Guinea, who shot the birds with bow and arrow and used their feathers in trade, prepared specimens by taking out the body, cutting off the legs, and then drying the skin over a fire. The Rajah of Batjan (who ruled the small Molluccan island of Tidore) presented several legless birds of paradise to El Cano, who had taken command of the great circumnavigation after Magellan's death. The birds reached Spain in 1522 and fostered the legend of ethereal, legless creatures that could not land and must come from paradise (hence their name). In 1551, Girolamo Cardano wrote: "Since they lack feet, they are obliged to fly continuously and live therefore in the highest sky far above the range of human vision. . . . They require no other food or drink than dew from Heaven." The Greater Bird of Paradise bears a technical name—crafted, in a fit of good humor, by the celebrated Linnaeus himself—to recall this oldest legend: *Paradisaea apoda*, literally, the legless [Bird of] Paradise.

The forty-or-so species of Birds of Paradise are members of the corvoid, or crow, lineage—a designation that sounds strange when we think of the raucous, unornamented, jet black birds that bear this name on northern continents. But the Corvoidea form an enormous group of predominatly southern hemisphere species, spanning a full range of form and behavior among songbirds; our common crow represents but a tiny and peripheral segment of this great radiation.

Birds of Paradise display beautiful colors in their plumage, but we celebrate them more for the form than the hue of their feathers. The diversity of shape and use is stunning. Some

46. Lyres of King-of-Saxony's Bird of Paradise

possess delicate fans and capes of fluffy spread (see photos 47 and 49). In others, only the shaft, or quill, of the feather remains—extended, gracefully twisted, and called a "wire" in appropriate reference to the closest analog of human construction. In *Parotia* (the Flagbird, or Six-Wired Bird of Paradise), six shafts extend in two groups of three from either side of the head. In the King Bird of Paradise (*Cicinnurus regius*) and the Magnificent Bird of Paradise (*Diphyllodes magnificus*), two wires extend from the rear (see photos 48, 51). In the strangest form of all, the small, thrush-sized King-of-Saxony Bird of Paradise, a pair of feathers extends back for more than 1½ feet from the head. Each feather (see photo 46) consists of a shaft bedecked on one side only, with some forty, silvery "flags."

(The name chosen for Birds of Paradise reinforce their gaudy majesty. Most were given monikers to honor various European monarchs. For example, the Blue Bird of Paradise, *Paradisaea rudolphi*, (see photo 47) honors the only son of Emperor Franz Joseph, the ill-fated Archduke Rudolph of Austria who, in frustration at his exclusion from government for his reformist ideas, committed suicide in 1889. One sharply noted exception, *Diphyllodes respublica*, was coined by the French ornithologist Charles Louis Bonaparte, nephew of the emperor. He chose his name, so he stated, because "I have not the slightest regard for the sovereignty of all the princes in the world." Yet he also thumbed his nose at earthly governments, selecting his label in mock honor of "that Republic which might have been a

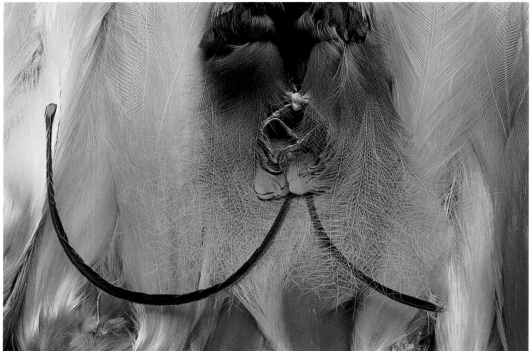

47. Birds of Paradise, arranged in order of geographical variation

Paradise had not the ambitions of Republicans, unworthy of the name they were using, made it by their evil actions more like a Hell.")

The key to the evolutionary meaning of these baroque conformations lies in two basic facts gleaned from the standard method of research in natural history: comparison among related species. (1) In highly ornamented species, only the males are so garbed. Females are plain and drab. Males play no role in building nests or rearing young. (2) In more ordinary species, males and females look much more alike and both participate in rearing the brood.

The correlation between male showiness and inactive fatherhood is scarcely accidental. The bedecked males congregate at display grounds called "leks." There they vie for female attention with elaborate rituals of calling and movement of plumes. Consider the personal observations of Tom Gilliard on the little bird with the long head feathers, the King-of-Saxony Bird of Paradise:

> The male was perched on a very thin, nearly horizontal
> limb. . . . With violent motions of the body it caused the
> perch to bounce up and down six or more inches. . . . As the
> bird bounced, the long plumes were brought forward and

48. Lyre from King Bird of Paradise

49. King Bird of Paradise

The Varied Facets of Paradise

50. Raggiana Bird of Paradise bound in bamboo

51. Bird of Paradise

The Varied Facets of Paradise

52. Albino Bird of Paradise

the head was repeatedly bowed forward and downward.
The bowing was a slow graceful sweeping motion. It was
repeated six or more times during the forty or sixty rapid
bounces that the bird was seen to execute. As the male
bounced and bowed, it kept up an almost constant hissing
like escaping steam.

The polygynous males thus attract and mate with as many females as possible in the great
Darwinian struggle for reproductive success. The males, having devoted all their effort and
energy to securing more copulations by showiness, play no further role in raising the next
generation. Males of the less ornamented species play their different version of Darwin's game
by mating with one female, putting all their fertilized eggs into one basket, and then protect-
ing the basket with zeal. Two strategies; same game: either protect one brood, or try to make
several and leave them to their fate, banking on a probability that some will survive.

Such bizarre and hypertrophied adaptations offer our best proof that nature operates in a
Darwinian fashion, and not by other evolutionary processes that might be more sensible or
benevolent in inappropriate human terms. These magnificent feathers and inordinately
complex display behaviors do no good for the species. Nor do they make a "better" bird in any
conventional sense. They are surely a burden with respect to daily chores of feeding and
flying. Think of the energy expended to build what are only ornaments; think of the days
passed in elaborate display, suited only to the luring of females and not at all to sustenance of
the body. But think of the radical message in Darwin's theory: natural selection is about
reproductive success, not "improvement" of design. Bizarre solutions that compromise the
longevity of a species, but aid an individual in the struggle for reproductive success, will
prevail in Darwin's world. Only in such a peculiar regime of causality — the regime actually at
work on our planet — could something so strange as a Bird of Paradise evolve.

So strange, but so suited to our parallel vanities. The Janissaries, élite corps of the Ottoman
Sultan's army, wore Bird of Paradise plumes in their ceremonial headgear as early as the
fifteenth century. But Victorian taste for filigree far outdid eastern arabesques, and the
women's hat trade of late nineteenth century finally converted feather hunting into big
business. The divisions of imperialism cut the New Guinea region into English, German, and
Dutch sections, and all three exploited the path from forest to headgear. At the height of the
trade, between the 1880s and World War I, up to 80,000 birds were killed and exported from
Dutch New Guinea per year. In 1912, a British firm received 28,300 skins in a single
shipment. As America had its boom and bust mining towns, New Guinea constructed its
feather settlements. Hollandia maintained a population of 700 in 1923 — Malay and Papuan
hunters, and Chinese, Arab, and Dutch traders. Ernst Mayr visited in 1928, following a ban
on hunting enacted in 1924; he found a ghost town with some 30 inhabitants.

Taxonomy has never been a munificently supported enterprise. Naturalists have lived by

53. Rothschild's Bird of Paradise

hook and crook, piggybacking on military expeditions, or hanging from the coattails of commercial enterprises. Many new species of Birds of Paradise were scrounged from traders' bins in Europe, not discovered by well-funded collecting expeditions in New Guinea.

Literature abounds with tales of instant conversion from squalor to splendor—Ralph Rackstraw to Captain of the *Pinafore*. Since life sometimes imitates art, even so untrendy a field as taxonomy finds its occasional angel. And what better go-between than a Bird of Paradise. No accident, then, that the most celebrated collector of these birds was the greatest private force that ever struck (and graced) natural history—Lord Walter Rothschild, scion of the great banking family.

Walter Rothschild (1868–1937) was a big man in every sense—from his person (he weighed more than 300 pounds), to his eccentricities (he loved to drive his four-in-hand of zebras right down Picadilly), to his wealth and resources, to his collections. He was titular chief of England's great banking family, and de facto head of Britain's Jewish community. The Balfour Declaration of 1917, promising British support for "the establishment in Palestine of a

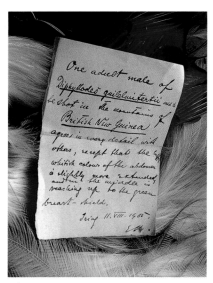

54. Hartet's note

national home for the Jewish people," was proclaimed not in a public document, but stated in a personal letter to Rothschild.

But Walter Rothschild found banking distasteful and felt indifferent to politics (though he worked hard for the declaration); his true love lay with natural history, primarily the taxonomy of butterflies and birds. When Chaim Weizmann, the Zionist leader, left for Palestine to see if he could facilitate the implementation of Balfour's declaration, Rothschild gave him another mission: "I want to find out what has become of two ostriches." (Rothschild had left the birds in care of a naturalist-schoolteacher near Jaffa and had lost contact with him during the disruptions of wartime). Weizmann dutifully located the ostriches, and Rothschild eventually described them as a new subspecies, *Struthio camelus syriacus*.

Walter Rothschild, with his unparalleled resources, built the largest collection in natural history ever assembled by one man. At times, he employed more than 400 collectors spread throughout the world. One cartographer, looking at a map with red dots marking Rothschild's sites of operation, said that it resembled "the world with a severe attack of measles." Rothschild built and maintained a museum at Tring (now run by the government as part of the British Museum). He stuffed the cases so full with the products of his indefatigable collecting that zebras and antelopes must be mounted in kneeling position, or even supine, so that one or two extra rows may be inserted to include all specimens in the floor-to-ceiling display.

But Walter Rothschild was not a mere gatherer or mindless collector interested only in augmenting his life list. He developed professional skills as a descriptive taxonomist, and his astounding eidetic memory enhanced his ability in this quintessentially comparative science. He established two of the world's finest taxonomists at Tring, E. Hartert and K. Jordan (a noble act of ecumenicism, especially amidst the jingoism of World War I, and for an English Jew, since both were German). He founded a journal, *Novitates Zoologicae*, to print their taxonomic results, and then he, and Hartert and Jordan, published and published and published—more than 5,000 new species and subspecies in 1,200 books and papers.

Moreover, the Tring trio were not mere describers, but thinkers and reformers as well. They advocated and developed the trinomial system (adding a third, or subspecific name to the Linnaean binomial to characterize geographic variation within species)—an important reform in the context of their time (though now largely superseded by our current ability to measure and map such variation in quantitative terms)—for trinomialism replaced the static, typological notion of species with a concept of dynamic and shifting boundaries (see photo 54, with Hartert's note, against a feathered background, about previously unrecognized variation in color within a Bird of Paradise species). For defining species, Rothschild always tried to amass large series, not just typical individuals (one reason for the burgeoning size of his collection), thereby reinforcing the cardinal evolutionary concept that variation is irreducible and the stuff of change.

Rothschild had a special fascination for Birds of Paradise. He wished to map and understand patterns of morphological variation, and geographic spread and overlap, within species of these most baroque birds. Over nearly forty years, Rothschild built by far the world's finest collection of Birds of Paradise, containing nearly every known species, including seventeen that he described for the first time. Ernst Mayr, who worked for Rothschild as a young man in the 1920s and 1930s (and who remains, in his mid-eighties, the world's leading ornithologist), remarked that Rothschild's collection was "of inestimable scientific value, because it contained large numbers of young, female, and male birds in various stages of molt, giving a complete picture of variation and evoluation in this wonderful group."

No man is an island unto himself, and no one can be fully insulated from the slings and arrows of outrageous fortune. Even the wealth of the Rothschilds could not hold the great Tring collection intact in the face of a lady's blackmail (documented but not detailed in the discreet sources now published on Rothschild's life and times). In 1932, Rothschild, with copious tears and great reluctance, offered his entire bird collection for sale. Mrs. Harry Payne Whitney bought it for the American Museum of Natural History in New York, where the Birds of Paradise now reside, and where Rosamond Purcell took these photographs.

The affinity seems so incongruous at first—these most delicate birds with this big, big, man of booming voice (through some defect of hearing or perception, Rothschild could not modulate his tones, and usually spoke as from a megaphone). But the meshing, in a deeper sense, could not have been better or more complete. Showy birds of opulent display with a man who could afford to collect their full variety. Delicate birds of exquisite design with a man who, despite external appearances, could not have been more courtly or gentle (Ernest Mayr remembers that Rothschild, feeling such deference before his curators, would never intrude upon their work, but would wait by the door until noticed and invited to enter). On second thought, everything fits. It was a marriage made in heaven.

NOTE: These birds come from the American Museum of Natural History, New York

6 RELICS OF THE FLOOD

*I*n 1695, John Woodward began his *Essay Towards a Natural History of the Earth* with a plea for observation over speculation as the watchword of a new scientific era: "From a long train of experience, the world is at length convinced, that observations are the only sure grounds whereon to build a lasting and substantial philosophy."

Woodward's treatise is a key document in one of the truly great, but little remembered, struggles in the history of ideas — the battle, if you will, for history itself. The debate centered on the nature and meaning of fossils, and the successful resolution established a chief signpost in our transition from Neoplatonism to the Cartesian (or Newtonian) world that has, forever since and for better or worse, shaped our destiny.

In 1664, the great Jesuit scholar Athanasius Kircher published his massive treatise on the earth and its objects (*Mundus subterraneus*), and interpreted fossils as manifestations of a plastic force inherent in rocks, not as the remains of ancient organisms. The detailed similarity between fossils and modern organisms, a sure sign of common genesis by modern standards, did not deter Kircher from his conclusion because a world pregnant with signs of unity among its different spheres (organic and inorganic, for example) would surely produce such examples of meaningful correspondence.

This neoplatonic theory of signs and correspondences engendered an attitude towards the earth that denied history as a source of explanation and therefore made geology, in any modern sense, impossible and irrelevant: the earth was made much as we find it now, with different powers and forces assigned to its diverse spheres (animals, vegetables, minerals), but with sufficient similarity among the products of all spheres to display a unity of purpose and design.

The revolution of Woodward and a host of contemporaries (including Leibniz, Hooke, Steno, and Scilla) gave the earth a sequential history: for if fossils are the remains of ancient organisms, then the rocks that form their tombs are made from sediments, and the layering of strata records a history of sequential events. The earth, in short, was built and altered step by step (whether gradually or with occasional violence)—not made in some admirable state and largely unchanged today.

To support his brave words about the primacy of observation, and to put money by his mouth, Woodward amassed the greatest geological collection in Britain—some 9,000 specimens, based largely on material personally collected in England, but greatly enhanced by specimens sent or purchased from friends and correspondents throughout the world. By provident planning, greatly abetted by good fortune in avoiding the pitfalls of war, fire, and simple neglect, Woodward's collection has retained (and enhanced) its preeminence by the simple strategy of fighting entropy and remaining intact—for almost all collections of his contemporaries have, long since, been dispersed or destroyed.

Upon his death, Woodward (1665–1728) left half his collection to Cambridge University, who then gave adequate signs of their serious intent by purchasing the other half for the substantial sum of £1000 even before the material came to auction. By terms of his will, Woodward also cleverly converted his estate into cash, purchased land with the bounty, and designated the income of that land to pay a lecturer (now the Woodwardian Professor, perhaps the most prestigious geological chair in England), who would also, among other duties, be required to curate and to display the collection.

Perhaps there shall not always be an England, but a social stability of 300 years has guaranteed the integrity of Woodward's collection. His specimens, still housed in their original (and gorgeous) antique cabinets, form the centerpiece of the Sedgwick Museum at Cambridge University. David Price, the current curator, estimates that the collections are 97–98 percent complete, as identified to the specimen by comparing the beautifully arranged objects in their original drawers (see photo 55) with entries in Woodward's published catalogs. catalogs. (See Price's excellent account in "John Woodward and a surviving British geological collection from the early eighteenth century," *Journal of the History of Collections*, volume 1, 1989, pages 79–95).

Woodward held—empiricists always do—that his particular theory of geological history arose by direct induction from his observations in the field and, particularly, from the specimens in his collection. (Woodward argued that Noah's deluge had suspended all sediments into a universal soup and that the entire stratigraphic record, with fossils entombed at various levels, represents a settling of layers in order of density, with heaviest material at the bottom of the pile. We may scoff at such a claim today, as John Ray did in Woodward's own time, but Woodward's theory had a powerful influence throughout Europe in fostering the intellectual transformation that established geology by reformulating the earth as a product of history). Woodward wrote, in the second paragraph of his 1695 treatise, thereby giving maximal prestige to the value of collections: "I shall in the work before me, give myself up to be guided wholly by matter of fact; . . . and not to offer anything but what hath due warrant

55. Agates from Woodward collection

from observations; and those both carefully made, and faithfully related." Needless to say, no theory, and surely not Woodward's fanciful account of Noachian power, emerges automatically from an objective study of rocks, or any other natural objects. As P. B. Medawar has written, "innocent, unbiased observation is a myth."

To expand beyond the borders of his green and pleasant land, Woodward obtained specimens from more than 150 colleagues—from Isaac Newton, John Locke, and Christopher Wren at home, to the buccaneer William Dampier, and William Byrd, the aristocratic Virginia planter and naturalist. But Woodward's greatest bounty derived from his purchase, in 1717, of the collection made in Malta, Sicily, and southern Italy by Agostino Scilla, an important though largely forgotten, figure in the genesis of geology.

Scilla was born in Messina, Sicily, in 1629 and died in Rome in 1700. He finished his education in Rome and then returned to Sicily. But his participation in the failed Messinian revolt against Spanish rule (1674–1678) forced him into permanent exile, first in Turin, and finally back in Rome. In 1670, Scilla published his important paleontological treatise, with its wonderful title, *La vana speculazione disingannata dal senso* (vain speculation undeceived by sense—that is, "by observation," not "by good thinking"). The frontispiece shows a young man of impressive solidity (representing observation), holding a fossil shark's tooth and sea urchin in one hand, pointing to a hillside draped in fossils with the other, and thereby instructing a floating wraithlike figure (representing speculation). In 1747, Scilla's treatise was republished in Latin under the less inspiring title *De corporibus marinis lapidescentibus* (On petrified marine bodies), but to greater effect as the work could now be read throughout the scientifically literate Western world (with its last universal language before the modern near-hegemony of English).

Scilla's argument is remarkably close to Woodward's, both in style and content—so much so that one of Woodward's critics came close to charging him with plagiarism in 1697. Scilla wrote his treatise primarily to argue for the organic nature of fossils against the neoplatonic claim that plastic forces of the mineral kingdom could produce objects with such stunning similarity to plants and animals. (Scilla's book takes the form of a letter addressed to the German neoplatonist and supporter of Paracelsus, Otto Croll). Scilla's fundamental appeal to sensation against speculation rests squarely upon his observations of fossils. He disclaims all interest in geological theories, as secondary and derivative (although he shared Woodward's conviction that fossils are products of the Flood; gave an even greater dimension to history by admitting the possibility of several successive floods each entombing fossils; and made many astute observations on stratification of rocks in Sicily, including the key recognition that numerous cycles of coarse to fine-grained sediments must indicate successive advances and retreats of water over the land). Scilla wrote:

> I have no idea how the sea could reach so far into the land; I
> do not know whether this happened during the universal
> Deluge or during other special floods. . . . I do not know,

neither do I know the way to find out. Nor do I care. What I do know is that the corals, the shells, the sharks' teeth, the dogfish teeth, the echinoids, etc., are real corals, real shells, real teeth; shells and bones that have indeed been petrified. . . . It seems to me impossible to arrive at any sort of knowledge of the truth if I abandon the path my eyes show me.

Scilla's last line—a sentiment oft repeated in his book—provides a clue to the special character that makes his work the most unusual of seventeenth century paleontological treatises, not just another entry in a long list of polemics on the contentious theme of the nature of fossils. Scilla writes frequently about the visual character of geological landscapes and fossil morphologies—and about the clues to scientific understanding that should derive

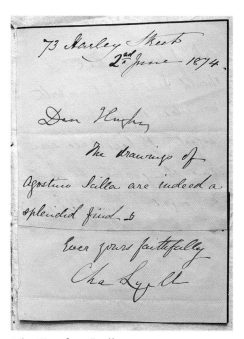

56. Note from Lyell

from insight literally won. And for good reason—because Scilla was a painter by profession, in fact one of the stars of the Sicilian *seicento*. (Such cross-disciplinary competence is not entirely extinct even today in an age of extreme specialization. Scilla's century, not so far removed from Leonardo as "*numero uno*" in both art and science, knew no restrictive boundaries of such later construction. The word "scientist" did not exist, and most great intellectuals strove for understanding, even for professional expertise, in a variety of truly related areas that, as the worst spinoff of increasing knowledge, later taxonomists of thought would artificially split asunder.)

Scilla used his artistic skill to draw not only the frontispiece of his work, but to engrave thirty beautiful plates at the end, figures that enhance the intrinsic beauty of fossils with an artist's sense of balance and placement (see photo 58). As a great blessing to a posterity that still cares for both truth and beauty (even if we allocate them to different faculties of universities), the Sedgwick Museum houses not only Scilla'a specimens, but also the original manuscript and drawings for the plates. Charles Lyell himself (see photo 56) commented on the "splendid find" of these original drawings.

Thanks to the kindness (and prior research) of David Price, we were able to compare Scilla's drawings with the original specimens still in the Woodwardian collection—thus to gain some

57. Urchin specimens

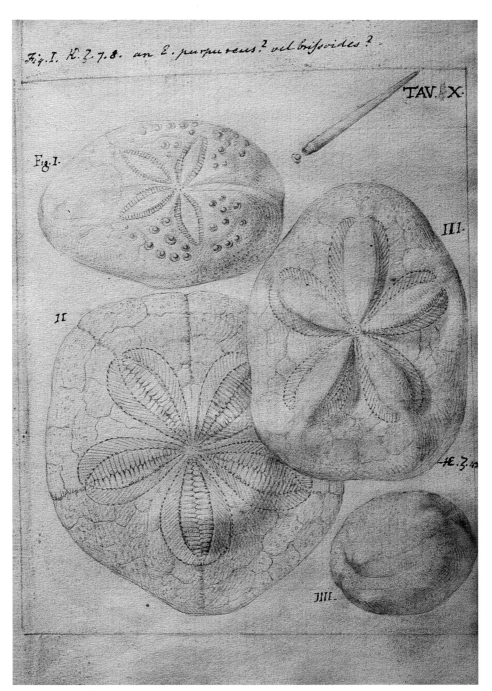

58. Drawing of Urchins

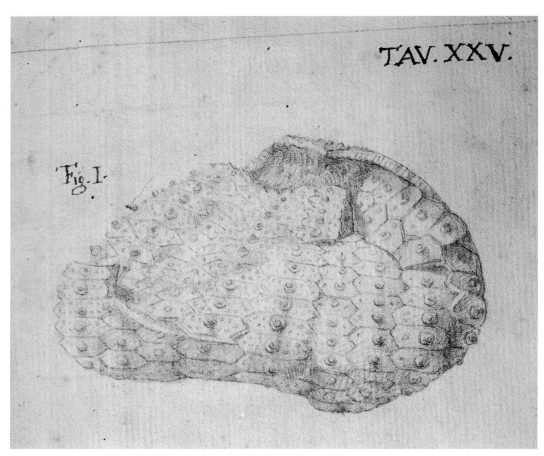

59. Drawing of echinoderm

60. Echinoderm depicted in drawing

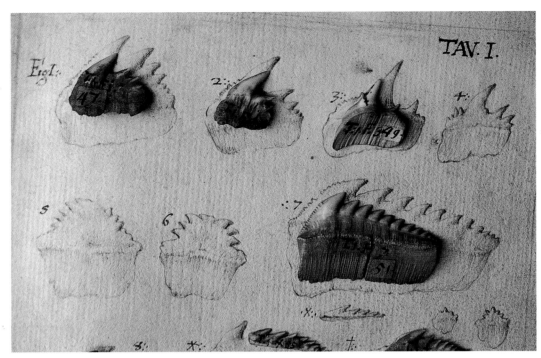

61. Shark teeth on drawing of the same teeth

insight into an early conjunction of art with science, and to obtain a precious opportunity for making a statement, both symbolic and concrete, about intellectual integrity.

Note, for example, Scilla's slightly crushed sea urchin drawn from the side, and known to the world for 300 years in this orientation only (photo 59). And now, observe the same specimen from the bottom (photo 60), with its identifying label in place—A. Scilla, T(able) xxv. f(igure) 1, with his home locality of Messina, written in old script with a gothic "s." Or note (photos 57 and 58) the two beautifully wrought urchins, compared with the actual specimens in the same orientation, but with their strikingly different surface textures (not so clear in the drawings).

Scilla's most important work lay in his resolution of the famous *glos-*

62. Drawing of a shark

63. Shark teeth

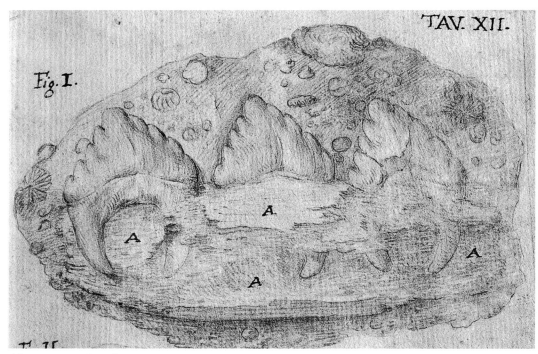

64. Drawing of shark's teeth

sopetrae (or tongue stones) of Malta as sharks' teeth (as the great Steno had done in his *Prodromus* of 1669, published a year before Scilla's treatise and apparently without his knowledge). The *glossopetrae*, known since Pliny's description and prominent ever after in all debates on the nature of fossils, had been interpreted in a variety of ways—as, for example, emanations from the sky during lightning storms, and as serpents' tongues following a curse that St. Paul had laid upon the vipers of Malta after he had received a bite when shipwrecked on his way to Rome. Scilla, using his method of visual comparison with teeth undeniably found in the mouths of modern sharks, ridiculed these legends and established the *glossopetrae* as true fossils and products of history.

In the light of Scilla's emphasis on visual accuracy, the subtle but systematic differences between drawings and specimens intrigue us. For example, Scilla elongated most of the multiply pointed teeth beyond their actual dimensions, perhaps to emphasize the distinctness of cusps. And he often "improved" incomplete specimens with reasonable inferences about actual absences—a point that Woodward noted with some annoyance, but with forgiveness. (Woodward wrote: "He took a little too much liberty in his Icon, there being several things in the Figure which are not in the Body. But indeed their [his critics'] Ill Usage and Exasperations of him, and his Zeal for maintaining his Argument, disposed him to take that Liberty

65. Shark teeth depicted in photo 64

in several other Particulars.") In one especially interesting example, Scilla portrays three teeth still affixed to the jaw of a shark. The raw drawing shows a completeness not evident in the specimen (photos 64 and 65), particularly in the tooth roots shown within the jaw. This fossil is crucial for two reasons—specifically, as a demonstration that "tongue stones" do sit in sequence within sharks' jaws, and must therefore be teeth; and, more generally, as a refutation of Kircher's theory of plastic virtues, for why should a rock grow fragments and torn pieces *sui generis*, while an actual organism will often be broken apart before burial. Interestingly, Benoit de Maillet used this very specimen as a key argument in his *Telliamed*, published in 1748 and presenting one of the earliest arguments for evolution (sufficiently controversial in his day that de Maillet published his work anonymously, as the supposed commentary of an Indian sage who just happened to bear a palindromic version of his own name). De Maillet wrote: "A remarkable example, illustrated in Scilla's dissertation, is that of a petrified jawbone with three of the teeth still attached to it. From this specimen, the author concludes that those which are found detached from their jawbone and inserted in these rocks, obviously have the same origin."

I am not bothered by these discrepancies of drawing and specimen. Rather I view the junction with a difference as a symbol of our entire enterprise in this book, for two things just alike are merely mirrors of each other. Instead, I look at the added dimension of the fossils themselves, and I contrast this literal depth with the increased clarity and instruction inherent in departures of the drawings (not to mention their overall beauty). I put one atop the other, both in my mind and in the pictures—and I see integrity with variety, the twin goals of our being bound into a single image.

7 JUDGMENT AND BRUTISH BEASTS

*I*n 1834, the eccentric and demented Thomas Hawkins extolled the virtues of untrammeled speculation, but then admitted the attendant difficulties, and finally concluded that a more focussed study of particular objects might yield even greater rewards:

> Oh the powers of the understanding, which dwells at the same moment with equal intensity upon an insect and a world! That considers the universe—worlds upon worlds—until, attempting infinity, its wings failing like those of Icarus, it drowns in the vasty deep of its own contemplative nothingness. Then the chastened soul seeks her accustomed channels and pensively attempts objects less calculated to confound her; then the mind's mood disposes it to enquire after more particular things, and to find out the circumstances which belong to them.

Hawkins chose, for his particulars, the abundant fossil ichthyosaurs and plesiosaurs of his native Somerset and adjacent Dorset. This driven man, who could do nothing by half, amassed a great collection "in the gratification," as he tells us, "of an inordinate acquisitive organ which understands no motive but curiosity." Hawkins hoped that the study of natural history would aid "the correction of the public taste," and he saw museums as the primary agent of reform:

> Let us haste then to found sumptuous museums, which shall be as sanctuaries for the arts—the divine arts—until ignorance, driven to herd with bats and owls and every unclean thing, ceases to persecute them:—and let us raise noble galleries to receive the spoils of invincible science.

Among the treasures of paleontology, some have been sought as longstanding objects of desire, and then discovered by expeditions sent to the ends of the earth (see Chapter 4 on Dubois and his quest for human ancestors in Indonesia). But others of no less import and beauty have been found as the business end of a stubbed toe in the backyards of the earliest paleontologists. The great marine reptiles of the Mesozoic era are not dinosaurs by technical definition, although all sets of plastic models, and all boxes of dinosaur pasta, chocolates, and cookies, include ichthyosaurs and plesiosaurs among the canonical forms, known (to the details of orthography, including the "chth" scourge of the spelling bee) by every five year old in America.

Limestones and marls, deposited in shallow oceanic waters during the age of dinosaurs, are abundant in southwestern England. Quarries for road metal and building stone, and natural erosion of sea cliffs, often exposed skeletons of the fishlike ichthyosaurs, and the long-necked plesiosaurs with tortoise–shaped bodies (prototype for the non-existent Loch Ness monster). At a time when mammals were mouse-sized creatures confined to the nooks and crannies of terrestrial life, these large marine reptiles formed a counterpart to dinosaurian domination on land (while the pterosaurs, yet another reptilian group, mounted a third phalanx of ascendancy in the air). For their abundance, their relative ease of collection, their minute detail, and their exquisite beauty, these marine reptiles became chief objects of desire and instruction when vertebrate paleontology arose as a modern science during the first third of the nineteenth century.

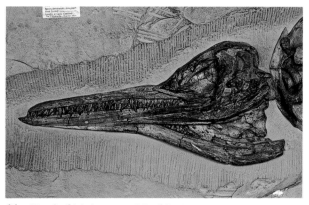

66. Head of ichthyosaur (Hawkins)

The astoundingly fishlike ichthyosaurs attracted particular attention and wonder. Their external form matched the design of a fish so intricately — the pointed snout (photo 66) recalling a marlin or swordfish, the sharply bent vertebral column extending into the lower portion of a two-lobed tail fin externally indistinguishable from that of an advanced bony fish (photo 70), above all, the limbs converted to swimming paddles (photos 75 and 69). And yet the reptilian prototype for the piscine modifications could not be denied; the paddles, for example, are built of conjoined fingers (not fish fin-rays), with the phalanges (finger bones) multiplied to long series of twenty or more (while we sport but two or three per finger) in order to elongate the digits to their required length as fin-ray analogs.

This status of "fish yet not-fish" inspired endless discussion among the early English paleontologists who studied ichthyosaurs with such zeal. The Reverend William Buckland,

67. Mouth spewing teeth (Hawkins)

first academic geologist of Oxford University (amidst his ecclesiastical duties), interpreted the uncanny likeness of ichthyosaur to fish as a proof of God's goodness. An ordinary reptile, Buckland acknowledged, would be in severe trouble at sea, but ichthyosaurs had been granted by divine fiat

> a union of compensative contrivances...so perfect in the adaptation of each subordinate part to the harmony and perfection of the whole; that we cannot but recognize throughout them all, the workings of one and the same eternal principle of Wisdom and Intelligence, presiding from first to last over the total fabric of the Creation.

On the other hand, the great anatomist Richard Owen, who was more interested in tracing the continuities of underlying structure than in discerning God in superficial adaptations, saw the retention of reptilian design as the main lesson to be learned from ichthyosaur skeletons. Noting that whales are also fishlike, but undoubtedly mammalian in structure, Owen wrote: "The adaptive modification of the Ichthyopterygian [ichthyosaur] skeleton, like those of the Cetacean [whale] relate to their medium of existence; [but] they are superinduced, in the one case upon a Reptilian, in the other upon a Mammalian type." (Evolutionary

68. Rib cage of ichthyosaur (Connybeare)

69. Ribs, backbone, and paddle

theory would later find the right concepts and terminology for these puzzles. Ichthyosaurs are reptiles by descent, and can never completely efface the complex signature of their ancestry. Their externally fishlike adaptations are evolutionary responses to their reinvasion of the seas. Swimming is a difficult art with few structural solutions; many independent lineages evolve similar forms in response to common environment—a phenomenon called "convergence.")

G. B. Shaw's famous dictum—"those that can, do; and those that can't, teach"—has an undeniably philistine component, but also captures an important truth. We might make a paleontological translation as "those who can, collect; and those who can't, interpret." Not fully fair, for some of the greatest theorists have also been fine explorers and field workers. But the valid sense honors the local amateur (in the literal sense of a word that means "to love")—the person who has walked over every square inch of surrounding territory and knows every stratum and every protruding bone (and who also serves as a compendium of practical knowledge about tides, thistle patches, bulls in fields, and appropriate bribes or sweet words for winning a farmer's heart and gaining access to private property). More often than not, the successful professional paleontologist is one who put in enough pub time to court and gain the loyalty of the local adept, not the lonely adventurer with naught but good eyes and a mediocre map. Yet the local collector (technically amateur, but fully professional in the sense of experience) usually disappears from historical accounts.

This theme gains its finest, and most colorful, illustration for the case of English ichthyosaurs and plesiosaurs. All the leading paleontologists of early nineteenth century England—Buckland, Conybeare, de la Beche, and others published copiously, and with great erudition, about these beasts; some of them even unearthed a specimen or two. But the great majority of important finds were made by two amateurs and local collectors who could not possibly have been more different in focus and temperament (even in gender)—the ultimate paleontological odd couple of Mary Anning, 1799–1847 (who lived and worked in the greatest fossil haven of Lyme Regis, site of John Fowles' paleontological novel, *The French Lieutenant's Woman*); and Thomas Hawkins, 1810–1889 (who grew up in Glastonbury, Somerset, worked mainly in the neighboring town of Street, but also collected extensively with Mary Anning in Lyme Regis). Rosamond Purcell and I felt that we had to honor this important tradition in a book about collectors—and we could neither find (nor even imagine) a better case than the fruitful contrast of Anning and Hawkins.

Mary Anning, probably the most important unsung (or inadequately sung) collecting force in the history of paleontology, was the daughter of a carpenter who supplemented his living, as so many citizens of Lyme Regis did (and still do), by selling shells and fossils to vacationers. When Anning was twelve, soon after her father's death, she found one of the first English ichthyosaurs in 1812. By good fortune, the naturalist Sir Everard Home was visiting Lyme Regis at the time, and encouraged Anning's work by praise for her industry and money for her specimen.

Remaining in the rich Liassic (Lower Jurassic) region of Lyme Regis all her life, Mary Anning made an astounding series of additional discoveries, including squidlike creatures

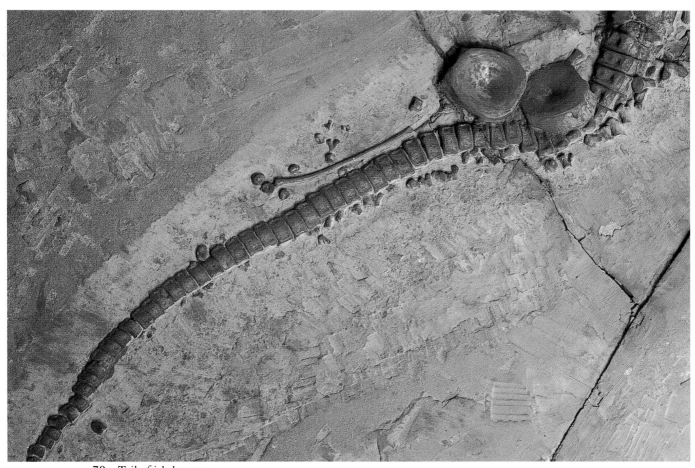

70. Tail of ichthyosaur

with associated ink-bags, a plesiosaur in 1824, and a pterosaur (flying reptile) in 1828 (photo 71 shows a starfish that she collected). The absolutely indispensable Anning received much praise in paleontological writings, but published nothing herself. One can almost play a game of "spot the Mary Anning encomium" in any British paleontological work about Liassic vertebrate fossils, for she directly found, or pointed the way to, nearly every specimen of importance. This, for example, on the first pterosaur from G. A. Mantell's *The Medals of Creation* (1844): "The most interesting British specimen...[was] found by Miss Mary Anning, whose indefatigable labors have been attended with such important results."

Mary Anning certainly knew her worth. One legend (probably true) holds that when the King of Saxony visited Lyme Regis, he stopped at the famous shop where Mary Anning sold her fossils. Anning, unperturbed and unsurprised, proceeded to tell the King that she was "well known throughout the whole of Europe."

We advance no profound social insight, but merely record an unfortunate, and widely recognized, truth in noting the difficulty of finding great female collectors to include in this book. Many women did take a strong interest in natural history, especially during the heyday of Victorian concern. But, as historian Lynn Barber points out, most female effort, given the strict limits of role divisions in a highly sexist society, went towards passive appreciation or beautification — "a solid undercurrent of female support which took tangible form in the shell pictures, seaweed albums, butterfly cases, and stuffed birds of the typical Victorian drawing-room." Almost no women published in technical journals. However, a middle ground did exist for a few driven and talented women, roles that did offer some professional reward, if not admission to scientific societies, or access to technical journals — dealing and collecting (also scientific illustration for others). Mary Anning was a paragon in this role, but other women made important contributions, most notably (for the same generation and subject matter as Anning), Ms. Elizabeth Philpott, also of Lyme Regis, and most accomplished of three naturalist sisters. We were delighted to find a beautiful picture of an ichthyosaur skull, drawn by Elizabeth Philpott "with color prepared from the fossil Sepia [squid] contemporary with the Ichthyosaurus." Since Mary Anning found the first fossil ink-sacs of squids, this drawing (photo 72) beautifully symbolizes, in uniting the efforts of these exemplary women, the struggles of half the human race to win respect for their interests.

71. Starfish (Mary Anning)

Thomas Hawkins, while not quite so precocious as Mary Anning, also developed his passion for ichthyosaurs and plesiosaurs at a tender age. He was elected a fellow of the

Geological Society of London at age twenty-two, and published, just two years later in 1834, the first of two large folio monographs replete with such florid language and such density of classical allusion that most readers would attribute a much greater age to its author.

Hawkins' enthusiasm for collecting the giant fossil reptiles was maniacal, in both technical and metaphorical senses. He describes his success in quarrying, with a posse of local workmen, a large ichthyosaur from surrounding sediment at Lyme Regis:

> Who can describe my transport at the sight of the colossus!
> My eyes the first which beheld it! — who shall ever see them
> lit up with the same unmitigated enthusiasm again! And I
> verily believe that the uncultivated bosoms of the working-
> men were seized with the same contagious feeling, for they
> and the surrounding spectators waved their hats to an
> hurra, that made hill and mossy dell echoing ring.

The work of a good collector—and Hawkins certainly ranks high within the category, whatever his eccentricities—does not end with freeing a specimen from an outcrop. The beautifully exposed skeletons of ichthyosaurs and plesiosaurs are products of months of labor— "preparation" in the jargon of naturalists. To prepare a specimen, Hawkins took mallet and chisel, and laboriously chopped matrix from specimen, exposing the bones (his modern successors use power tools, including dental drills for the finer work). Note Hawkins' elegant sculpting with hammer and chisel in photo 67. Moreover, the seaside marls (home of many fine

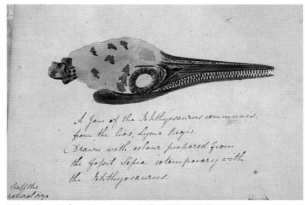

72. Fossil drawing in sepia by Miss Philpot

specimens) are finely cracked and poorly consolidated; they may crumble to powder as they dry, consigning the equally friable bones to the same fate. Thus, Hawkins had to "babysit" some specimens for weeks as they dried, applying various glues and gums to prevent cracking and powdering. He writes of his effort with one difficult specimen that had begun to fall apart:

> I shall never forget the intense heat of the following fort-
> night during which time, the Sabbath excepted, I was
> engaged from daylight to darknight [a lovely neologism] in
> developing it. The heat did I say, — yea, the heat of the

73. Vertebrae and paddle of ichthyosaur

blessed sun, for by that was dried, against the brick-walls
of my work-house, the Acacian gum with which I succeeded in reintegrating it. Had not this warm weather
fallen out, all my pains must have been abortive.

Hawkins' collection grew apace. The totality was not nearly so monumental as his own ego,
but Hawkins' zeal had been amply rewarded. Hawkins wrote in 1834:

The collection . . . weighs more than twenty tons, occupies
a superficies of two hundred feet by twenty, and, in preten-
sion of every sort, transcends all the collections in the
world [he means, I trust, of ichthyosaurs and plesiosaurs].
The suspicion of egotism is contemptible — the reader will
understand me when I tell him that the sight of about a
tenth part of the Collection, which I brought to London
two years ago, surprised and delighted so much the most
distinguished geologists of our time that I was encouraged
to humor my oryctological [an old word for "paleontological"] hobby until it secured me the most valuable aggrega-

74. Scattered bones

tion of fossil organic remains extant. This stupendous
treasure was gathered by me from every part of England;
arranged, and its multitudinous features elaborated from
the hard limestone by my own hands.

Eventually, even Hawkins had to let go and contemplate sale or donation to the museums that he loved so well: "I went on, gathering one rarity after another, as a second Cheops with a million slaves at his imperial beck and might, until, in 1833, my Collection exceeded all powers of accommodation and obliged me to contemplate the disposal of it." Hawkins therefore sold two major lots to the British Museum in 1834 and 1840 and, later, donated large suites of skeletons to both Oxford and Cambridge universities. Rosamond Purcell used Hawkins' specimens at the Sedgwick Museum, Cambridge University, for the photographs of this chapter.

In addition to, and ultimately overarching, all the complex themes of enthusiasm, energy, and egotism that marked Hawkins' (larger than) life, we must face the tragedy of his probable madness—for his eccentricities go far beyond the pleasurable English stereotype into the realm of tortured insanity. My colleague Michael Taylor, a leading ichthyosaur expert of our generation, notes that Hawkins was "certainly unpleasant, litigious, and probably insane." A

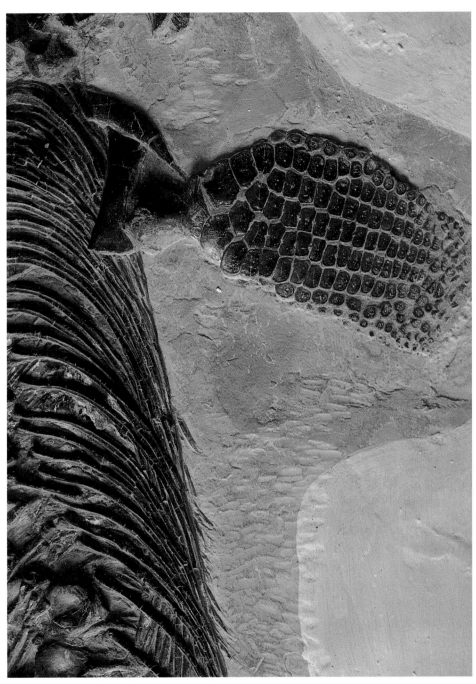

75. Ribs and paddle of icthyosaur (Hawkins)

biographic note (1970) from the *Central Somerset Gazette* concludes: "He was very eccentric, conceited, and pugnacious, and his chief hobbies were quarreling and fighting law-suits." His life, poorly documented though it be, consists largely of litigations and delusions. In one inadequately attested (though likely true) story, Hawkins—with customary zeal and tenacity —sued a transport company over a two pence error in billing made by a clerk. In another, he fancied himself the rightful Earl of Kent and made himself a seal replete with heraldic devices.

But the internal evidence of his two monographs is enough to sustain the suspicion of insanity. He often writes of self-tortures imposed by his own raging emotionalism, as in this passage on his fear that a high tide might destroy a specimen that he had been excavating:

> How often have I reflected upon the very-Bedlam-impetuosity of my passions at that moment:—the sea rolling over an Ichthyosaurus and remorselessly tearing it to a thousand atoms—a superb skeleton of untold value triturated to sand by a million pebbles, such was the Promethean idea—torture of my rebel imagination.

(Fear not; Hawkins successfully collected the skeleton at the next low tide.)

Hawkins clearly worsened during the 1830s as he made his great collection. The two monographs of 1834 and 1840 display a mind in disaggregation. The 1834 work, source of all previous quotes, is florid enough, but still tractable. The 1840 text is all but unreadable, as its final words attest (ostensibly about the future battle of angels against Gog and Magog that will end the Millennium, or thousand-year reign of Christ—and the knowledge of more ancient battles that these angels will obtain when they find the bones of ichthyosaurs and plesiosaurs, dragons of the pre-Adamic age):

> The baneful Dragons, O Seas, are gone: Friends O Earth, have filled thee with the bones of Defeat and Death. Future Angels to whom the Wars and Destructions of Time are unknown, shall seek throughout the limitless Empires of Space their ghastly remains, and finding amongst them the self-same Weapons of which we speak, be curious in remote centenaries to hear anew the Tale of the Dragons.

And, for a dramatic visual illustration of Hawkins' growing instability, compare the frontis-pieces of the two monographs (see photos 76 and 77)—the 1834 version with dignified, well-separated creatures going about their daily business, and the 1840 scene of twisted, writhing death and destruction.

In the Hollywood genre of "buddy" or "odd couple" movies, the mismatched members of the pair must meet and work together. Anning and Hawkins, the two greatest collectors of ichthyosaurs, did indeed collaborate on Hawkins' frequent collecting trips to Lyme Regis. Hawkins describes their interaction in detail in his 1834 monograph. He begins with the customary praise that all writers heaped upon Mary Anning. Hawkins notes the influence of professional researchers on his work — Conybeare, Buckland, and de la Beche — but he singles out Mary Anning as even more important:

76. Serene ichthyosaurs. Frontispiece of first monograph

77. Furious ichthyosaurs. Frontispiece of second monograph

> But, although many obligations are owing to the zealous efforts of these justly eminent personages, yet it must never be forgotten how much the exertions of Miss Anning, of Lyme, contributed to assist them. This lady, devoting herself to science, explored the frowning and precipitous cliffs there, when the furious spring-tide conspired with the howling tempest to overthrow them, and rescued from the raging ocean, sometimes at the peril of her life, the few specimens which originated all the fact and ingenious theories of these persons.

Thereafter, however, while remaining generous in his praise, Hawkins uses Anning primarily as a literary foil to contrast her caution with his victorious impetuosity. Anning, for example, doubts that some fragments will lead to a complete skeleton, but Hawkins persists and triumphs: "Persuaded that the other portions of the skeleton must be there, I advised its extrication, if it were possible, but Miss Anning had so little faith in my opinion, that she assured me I was at liberty to examine its propriety or otherwise for myself."

On another occasion, Anning advises that a skeleton cannot be collected because it will fragment to splinters and powder, but Hawkins again demurs:

> "You will never get that animal," said Miss Anning, as we made our devious way towards Lyme through the mist and

flashing spray, "or if you do, per-chance, it cannot be saved." My eyes glare upon the intellectual countenance before me, — the words on those lips were, I knew, oracular as those of a Pythoness and my heart fainted within me. . . . As Miss Anning had anticipated, the marl— as soon as it dried—cracked, but by the assistance of some clever carpenters we secured it in a tight case with plaster of Paris so that no power can now disturb it.

A primal theme of human conflict in relationships, is it not? Caution vs. daring; angels not treading and fools rushing in; conservative and radical; classical vs. romantic; always successful but limited vs. expansive with frequent failure. As with all the yins and yangs of life, we probably need both to cover any ground completely. And yet, as I survey the specimens in our photographs, I cannot help but feel that Mary Anning holds the upper hand —as least in consonance of her vision with the animals of their joint interest. Look at the bones. Did ever you see a more elegant, a more stately, a more severely geometric set of abstract forms? Dark against dark; clean lines; primary shapes. The perfect circles of the vertebral disks against the smoothly curving arches of the ribs. The paddles at right angles to the vertebral column, itself composed of a score of disks on strict parade. The finger bones of the paddles, arranged in rows, with individual phalanges in hexagonal closest packing about their fellows—the ideal geometry for filling space by complete tessellation. Thomas Hawkins' formless insanity secured these specimens; Mary Anning's stately order prevails.

NOTE: The starfish belonging to Mary Anning comes from The British Museum of Natural History, London. The ichthyosaur specimens come from the Sedgwick Museum, Cambridge, England, and from the University Museum, Oxford.

8 FISHES IN AND ON STONE: AGASSIZ'S TREASURES NOW AND THEN

*W*hen I saw the gleaming steel axes, the shining locomotives, and the gaily painted trade signs in the Smithsonian's reconstructed Philadelphia Centennial Exposition of 1876, I understood something important about our misperception of Victorian America. My vision of this age as uniformly drab and dour had largely been created by the subsequent decay and disrepair of its artifacts, not the temper of the time itself. (I had experienced much the same insight when I first saw brightly painted medieval statues in the Dahlem Museum of Berlin.)

We face a similar problem in understanding great works from the history of science. We view them as archaic, and they become collectibles for antiquarians. If they contain beautiful illustrations, as so many classics of natural history do, they become *objets d'art*, and leave the realm of science altogether (at least by the light of our false taxonomy that divides rational science from intuitive art).

Yet these works, in their own time, were the shiny tools of forefront science and their detailed, accurate, colorful illustrations were not drawn only to sell copies, but to express the inner workings of science itself. When we grasp the proper role of these illustrations, we can both appreciate the true status of great works in natural history, and also identify the deep error in our conventional separation of art and science.

Louis Agassiz (1807-1873) was the dominant figure of nineteenth century American biology. As the first great academic naturalist to leave Europe and make his permanent home in America, he fueled and superintended our transition from colonial outpost to scientific center. His European reputation rested upon two primary achievements—his formulation of the theory of ice ages (*Études sur les glaciers*, 1840), and his magnificent compendium on all known fossil fishes (*Les poissons fossiles*, 1833-1843).

Les poissons fossiles is a premier example of a work doomed to later misunderstanding by the differential aging of its text and illustrations. This great monograph was an integral work, both in Agassiz's mind and in the judgment of his contemporaries. Text and plates had appeared in dribs and drabs throughout the 1830s, causing complaint and frustration among Agassiz's subscribers. Finally, in 1843, Agassiz put everything together into five volumes of text (one for introduction and one each for the four orders in his chosen taxonomy), and an accompanying compendium of 391 plates, enormous in both size and number. (Agassiz tried to draw his fishes at their natural size—as Audubon did for birds—though he compromised and allowed some reductions for a few aquatic giants.)

Agassiz's text may be the founding document for our small company of paleoichthyologists (students of fossil fishes, for those untutored in our jargon), but it has otherwise passed into oblivion. We regard Agassiz's taxonomy (based on shape and composition of scales) as erroneous and outdated, and his defense of creationism runs squarely against the later discoveries of Darwin's world. Yet, as his text became more and more irrelevant, his plates have increased enormously in value to a different company of art collectors, and complete copies can now command close to five figures.

This modern perception of beautiful plates encumbered by a massive and inaccessible text (*en français*), completely misrepresents *Les poissons fossiles* as perceived in its own time. The plates, as an early example of chromo, or color lithography, are an artistic innovation in themselves (older works of natural history are almost invariably hand colored). Their accuracy and beauty had aesthetic and commercial motives to be sure. (Massive monographs like this were funded by private subscriptions paid in advance, and pretty plates undoubtedly boosted sales.) But the primary justification for large illustrations of such intricate detail was intellectual and scientific.

In the 1830s (it is no different today), fossil fishes lay scattered in scores of collections, both in public museums and private cabinets. To write a complete monograph, Agassiz had to compare all these specimens. But he could not bring them to his home in Neuchâtel. As Muhammad had deferred to the mountain, Agassiz had to visit the fishes in their own domain —and proper comparison required images of fossils from other places. Since neither the mind nor the infant art of photography were adequate, Agassiz relied (as did all naturalists involved in such a task) upon portfolios of scrupulously accurate drawings. In other words, the drawings that became, via lithography, the plates of *Les poissons fossiles* were the primary working tools of Agassiz's science, not some fluff added later for the sake of art and commerce. They were both his centrifuge and his computer.

This comparison with the tools of bright, young, modern biologists on the make is quite appropriate—for Agassiz was a passionate, ambitious neophyte on a conscious quest both for personal recognition and for scientific understanding. (We contrast these two goals in disingenuous pronouncements about the norms of science, but they have never been dissociated in fact.) If we view *Les poissons fossiles* as the faded relic of a bygone age, we will not understand it. I suggest that we regard Agassiz as the Watson and Crick of his day, coursing through Europe in search of fame and the secret of life — and using the newest methods of science at its cutting edge.

Consider the context. The science of paleontology was in its infancy. George Cuvier, Europe's greatest natural historian, had only established the fact of extinction in 1812. (Before then, many scientists believed that all fossils represented species still living, and that our geological archives therefore recorded no sequential history of life or time at all.) No group of fossil vertebrates had ever been monographed *in extenso* (Cuvier had devoted most of four volumes in *Les ossemens fossiles* to mammals, but had only scratched the surface). Agassiz, filled with the ambition and energy of youth, jumped into an impossible task and nearly succeeded (Agassiz reluctantly pulled his work together in 1843 with a few specimens and plates outstanding. As they still say in the trade, a few of the big ones got away).

One fact will illustrate the magnitude of Agassiz's accomplishment. *Les poissons fossiles* describes some 1,700 species based on more than 20,000 specimens. This single monograph, devoted to fishes alone, increased by more than tenfold the total number of *all* vertebrate fossil species formally described before Agassiz began his work.

Agassiz's age considered taxonomy the most noble and important of all natural sciences — for the interrelationships of organisms reflected the structure of their creator's mind and provided, perhaps, our best insight into the nature of divinity. Yet interrelationship through time, as recorded by fossils, had been the central ingredient previously missing. Proper taxonomy was the route to life's innermost secret. Agassiz had done something truly extraordinary; he had not merely described a bunch of fishes.

Agassiz's father — was it ever different — had primed his son to become a doctor, but Louis longed for a career in natural history. When, at age twenty-two, Louis published his first monograph on the fishes of Brazil, he wrote with pride to his sister Cécile: "Already forty colored folio plates are completed. Will it not seem strange when the largest and finest book in Papa's library is one written by his Louis?") Six months later he carried his plea directly to Papa — and won: "Here is my aim and the means by which I propose to carry it out. I wish it may be said of Louis Agassiz that he was the first naturalist of his time, a good citizen, and a good son, beloved of those who knew him. I feel within myself the strength of a whole generation to work toward this end." These are not the dreams of a simple cataloguer, diligent at best, who merely wanted to list, draw, and order the world's fishes!

Louis' first comment to sister Cicile underscores the central role of illustration in his research. Agassiz's work on fishes, from 1828 until his departure for America in 1846, was a partnership with artists, primarily with one man — Joseph Dinkel — who drew about 80 percent of the plates for *Les poissons fossiles* (they were then lithographed by others), and who worked continually for Agassiz throughout the years of his European triumphs.

Dinkel first joined Agassiz's payroll in 1828, when Agassiz was still a student in Munich (not impoverished to be sure, but scarcely well-heeled). Agassiz wrote of his student life in

Munich: "I kept always one and sometimes two artists in my pay; it was not easy, with an allowance of $250. a year, but they were even poorer than I, and so we managed to get along together." In thus spending for his science absolutely every *Pfennig* beyond the bare necessities of food and lodging, Agassiz began a pattern that would inspire and enrage friends and associates throughout his life. Any monies that came in went out immediately to buy that collection, engrave these plates, or publish this work. (Louis never secured the finances of his Museum. We remain solvent today because his son Alexander struck it rich in mining while furthering his father's work in natural history).

Agassiz's insistence on employing Dinkel from his meager student's stipend was a consistent and primary source of friction with his parents. When Louis finally returned home in 1830, to consolidate his work and fortune, he wrote to his father: "I shall not bring any friend with me. I long to enjoy the pleasures of family life. I shall, however, be accompanied by one person....He is the artist who makes all my drawings." Papa replied tersely, and with emphasis: "Give all possible care to your affairs in Munich, put them in perfect order, leave nothing to be done, and leave nothing behind *except the painter*." (Dad finally relented and found Dinkel an apartment in town, while refusing to lodge him *chez lui*).

Agassiz's mixture of zealous idealism with a keen sense of practical and personal ambition (not to mention the prerequisite of keen intelligence) both secured his fame in general, and won the rights, by a clever tactical maneuver, to write *Les poissons fossiles*. Agassiz longed and lusted after this dream project of a lifetime—to write a monograph on all fossil fishes. But he faced a formidable obstacle. Georges Cuvier, the greatest and most politically powerful naturalist in the entire world, sat in Paris with plans well advanced and partly executed for the very same project. How could Agassiz, little known at age twenty-three, outflank the man acclaimed as the Aristotle of his day? Agassiz devised a bold plan and pulled it off, with Dinkel as the trump card.

Agassiz knew that he would have to assault Cuvier sweetly in his own lair. He had a leg up already, for Cuvier had admired Agassiz's first effort on Brazilian fishes. Agassiz therefore set out for Paris, with Dinkel—but not by a direct route. To his parents' consternation (for Louis had less money than ever and had been funded for his Parisian trip by a generous family friend), he stopped for many months at several German museums with good collections of fossil fishes that Cuvier had never seen. He described these fishes and made sure that Dinkel drew them with special care and elaboration. He then arrived in Paris, begged an audience with Cuvier, and showed the great man his work: "I hastened to show my material to M. Cuvier the very day after my arrival. He received me with great politeness, though with a certain reserve."

Agassiz, with a mixture of charm, intelligence, and tactics that only a master like Cuvier could appreciate, soon succeeded beyond his wildest dreams (or so the usual cliché goes, but I should say "soon succeeded exactly as he had dared to hope and plan"). Cuvier, knowing that he was too old and too burdened with other projects to finish the fossil fishes, and perceiving

78. Fossil fish, Lyme Regis

in Agassiz both the zeal and loyalty for such a task, resigned in Agassiz's favor and entrusted to Louis' care all the manuscript and figures that he had already prepared. Three months later, Agassiz went to the Paris Museum one Sunday morning and found Cuvier at work on another small project. Cuvier passed this research to Agassiz as well, saying "You are young; you have time enough for it, and I have none to spare." The next day, Cuvier, wearing his political hat, collapsed in the Chamber of Deputies, and was taken home to die.

Agassiz always attributed his success with Cuvier—the turning point of his professional life—to the excellence of Dinkel's work. Since Agassiz was poorer than ever in Paris, his mother again raised the sore subject of Dinkel's salary and begged: "My last topic is Mr. Dinkel. You are very fortunate to have found in your artist such a thoroughly nice fellow; nevertheless, in view of the expense, you must make it possible to do without him . . . . It is a great evil to be spending more than one earns." Agassiz refused again, replying:

"As my justification for having engaged him in the first instance, and for continuing this expense till now, I can truly say that it is in a great degree through his drawings that M. Cuvier has been able to judge of my work, and so has been led to make a surrender of all his materials in my favor. I foresaw clearly that this was my only chance of competing with him, and it was not without reason that I insisted so strongly on having Dinkel with me. . . .Had I not done so, M. Cuvier might still be in advance of me."

The symbiosis of Agassiz with Dinkel and a corps of additional artists and lithographers continued throughout the decade of subsequent work on *Les poissons fossiles*. When Agassiz, hoping that his labors were drawing to a close, found in England more than twice as much material as he had seen before, it was Dinkel who then lived there for seven full years in order to complete the figures. When Agassiz became frustrated by the difficulties and expense of shipping material back and forth between Neuchâtel and Munich for lithography, he established his own printing firm and lithographic press in his home town. He also lodged and fed his artists and lithographers in his own home, turning his research into a true industry and obsession. The entire process of illustration—from first drawing through final lithographic plate in color—became for *Les poissons fossiles* what the complete armamentum of a modern laboratory is to any modern molecular biologist. Illustration—the *process* as well as the product —is an indispensable key for understanding the *science* of natural history.

In planning this book on collectors, Rosamond and I decided that a comparison of Agassiz's original plates with the actual specimens—for many, if not most, can be found in modern museums might be both instructive and appealing, for specimens and published illustrations form the primary symbiosis (but not without tension) in the profession of natural history. Rosamond therefore visited the British Museum, source of Agassiz's most important material and, with the kind help of keeper Colin Patterson, photographed Agassiz's specimens.

We present five pairs below. We choose these five to represent the largest possible range of rock textures and types of fishes—in order to provide a spectrum of comparisons between illustrations and actual specimens. We refrain from much commentary because such contrasts are perhaps best (and most broadly) made without too much direct guidance. But we noted most how much richer the texture and dimensionality appear in the specimens, while the plates convey more precision and detail in outlines and parts of fishes. This last statement may seem paradoxical since we tend to regard photographs of things themselves as truer and more direct than drawings. But scientists continue to prefer drawings to photographs in many circumstances today because only drawings can present, by line and emphasis, the intricate features of many complex organisms (without altering proportions or colors). Indeed, the forefront of current advance in paleontological photography has centered upon the development of new techniques in illumination and coating (liquids and powders), designed to bring out details that, heretofore, could only be captured by drawings.

79. *Cephalaspis lyelli*: Fossil

Agassiz described this fish as "the most curious animal that I have ever observed. Their characteristics are even so extraordinary that I required the most attentive and scrupulous study, and the most persuasive proofs, to convince me that these mysterious animals are really fish." The crescent-shaped head shield, usually found detached from the body, had been previously described as a trilobite mouth part (the superficial similarity is great indeed), but when Agassiz found these pieces articulated to a body with scales, he made his correct taxonomic placement.

Cephalaspis is an agnathan, a member of the most ancient group of jawless fishes (only the lamprey and hagfish survive today) that served as ancestors to all later vertebates. (Agassiz found no jaws, but was not ready to accept the radical—and correct—conclusion that they truly had none. He assumed that better preserved specimens would provide evidence for jawbones sometime in the future.)

The British continue to use some delightful vernacular terms for their geological formations. This specimen (Devonian in age) comes from the Old Red Sandstone (*Vieux grès rouge* to Agassiz)—a quarryman's term for the oxidized coarsely grained, and terrestrially deposited

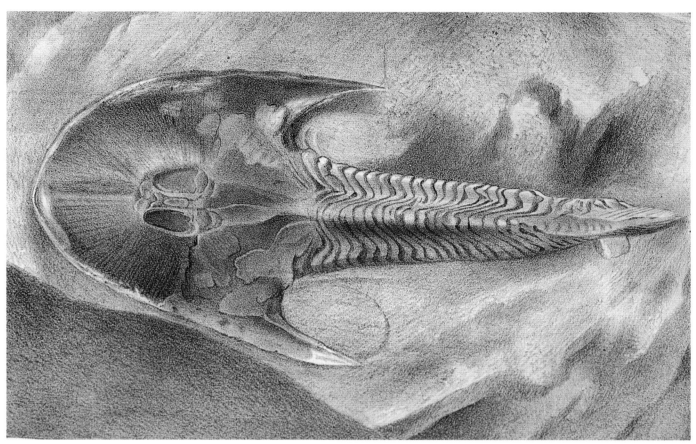

80. *Cephalaspis lyelli:* Lithographic plate

sandstone that usually underlies coal-bearing strata in Britain. By overlaying colors of slightly different hue, the new technique of chromolithography could capture the subtle textures of the Old Red far better than any previous method of reproduction. But note the richer variegation of the original...and note how the specimen lies *in* the rock while, in the lithograph, it appears *on* the rock.

Charles Lyell, personal friend and intellectual opponent of Agassiz, and perhaps the greatest geologist of all time, gave this Scottish specimen to Agassiz for description. Agassiz returned the favor by naming the species in Lyell's honor.

SECOND PAIR. *Beryx germanus* (photos 81 and 82)

81. *Beryx germanus:* Lithographic plate

The Old Red is an ancient formation, some 400 million years old. This specimen, by contrast, comes from the Chalk, last formation of the Mesozoic Era ("age of dinosaurs," which ended some 65 million years ago, perhaps with a bang). The Chalk, often stark white (though not in this German specimen), blankets much of Western Europe (forming, for example, the White Cliffs of Dover). It is often soft and crumbly, preserving its fossils exquisitely, with maximal contrast — accentuated in the lithograph —between organism and rock.

This is the only specimen in this chapter not drawn by Dinkel. The noted German paleontologist Goldfuss gave this specimen to Agassiz for description and also had it drawn by his own artist. The collaboration of Goldfuss and Hohe (his artist) was as fruitful as that of Agassiz and Dinkel—for Hohe executed the plates of Goldfuss's great monograph on the fossils of Germany.

82. *Beryx germanus:* Fossil

83. Fossil: *Eugnathus ortheostomus*

 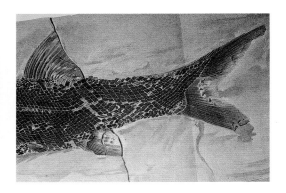

84. Lithographic plate: *Eugnathus ortheostomus*

"Ce magnifique poisson" (this magnificent fish), Agassiz tells us, comes from lower Jurassic shales of Lyme Regis in southern England, one of the world's most famous spots for collecting fossils (and favorite haunt of many paleontologists, from Mary Anning, England's great discoverer of dinosaurs and their kin [see Chapter 7] to fiction's most celebrated student of fossils, the hero of John Fowles' *French Lieutenant's Woman*). This large specimen, beautifully preserved in its fine-grained sediment, appears full sized in a large fold-out plate of *Les poissons fossiles*. We present its front and back separately.

FOURTH PAIR. *Palaeorhynchum latum* (photo 85 and 86)

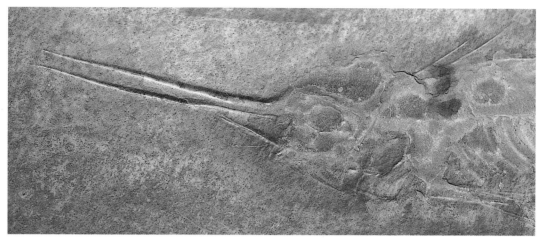

85. *Paleorhynchyum latum:* Fossil

When a slab is split to reveal a fossil on a bedding plane, we often obtain two specimens for our collections — one (the "part") containing the bone or shell of the organism itself, the other (the "counterpart") preserving the impression made by the organism's remains upon the overlying sediment. The ghostly appearance of the original in this pair reflects its status as the counterpart to the specimen used to draw the plate. In addition, preservation is poor in these rocks (the Glaris slates) because heat and pressure have metamorphosed the original sediments, partly destroying the fossil and blurring the distinction between animal and sediment. Drawings show their superiority to photos as scientific tools in such situations.

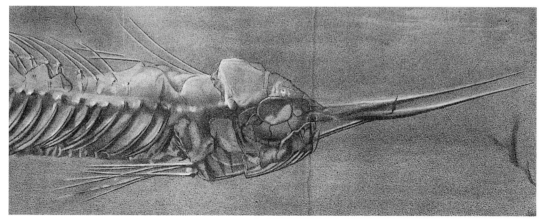

86. *Paleorhynchyum latum:* Fossil

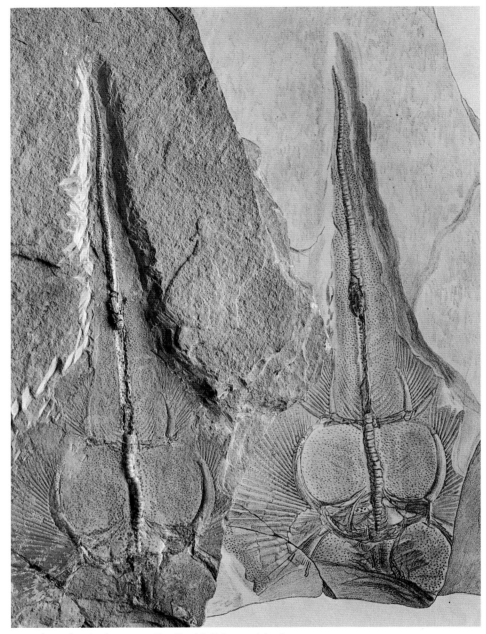

87. *Asterodermis platypterus:* Fossil with lithographic plate

A small fossil ray from the most exquisite of all spots for collecting fossils—the quarries of Solnhofen, Germany. This last figure embodies an interesting recursion that can serve as an epilogue and ending to this chapter. Rocks from the Solnhofen quarries are called "lithographic limestone" because virtually all the world's fine lithographs, including the plates of *Les poissons fossiles*, have been, and continue to be, drawn on these stones. ("Lithography," by etymology, means "writing on stone.") The same evenness and fineness of grain that makes this rock so suitable for art has also permitted the exquisite preservation of its fossils. Besides these lovely fishes, Solnhofen stones have also yielded the only specimens of the first bird *Archaeopteryx*, complete down to the fine details of feather barbs. So fossil becomes art drawn on the rock that contains fossil.

Lithography was also the primary cause of Agassiz's European undoing and his decision to relocate in America—so we should be thankful for parochial reasons, since Agassiz then set the course of natural history in America (see Chapter 9). The two primary causes for his move were sad—bankruptcy and the wreckage of his first marriage.

The poignancy is well recorded by a little hint in the plates of *Les poissons fossiles*. The left corner of two lovely plates, bears the identification "C. Agassiz, del."—drawn by (from the Latin *delineare*) Cécile Agassiz, Louis' first wife. Cécile worked with her husband at first, but became increasingly estranged as *Les poissons fossiles* became an obsession continually ranked before family—and when family life itself expired in its own domicile as Agassiz brought the personnel of his lithographic press to live and eat in his home. Cécile finally left, and moved with their children back to her parent's home. Soon thereafter, Agassiz's lithographic business went bust. The offer of a fat lecturing fee from the Lowell Institute in Boston, with added support from some aristocratic backers in Europe, made a trip to America too tempting to resist, especially in the light of his twin debacles at home.

The standard biographies of Agassiz record his joy and sense of renewal in his departure for America. But we must not neglect his sadnesses. Primarily, of course, he had left his children behind, in the care of his wronged, estranged, and still beloved wife (who would die two years later of tuberculosis). But his most important partner, Joseph Dinkel, also decided to remain in Europe, despite Agassiz's entreaties that he uproot once more and come to America.

Dinkel outlived Agassiz and, as an old man, wrote—in somewhat broken English, still remembered from those seven years spent drawing fishes in London—a letter of condolence to Elizabeth Cary Agassiz, Louis' second wife and founder of Radcliffe College. He recalled his sadness at their separation after eighteen years of symbiosis: "For a long time I felt unhappy at that separation. . . . He was a kind, noble-hearted friend . . . if he had possessed millions of money he would have spent them for his researches in science."

Dinkel also recalled the ambition and ardor of his old boss: "Often, when he saw a number of students going off on some empty pleasure trip, he said to me, 'There they go with the other fellows; their motto is, "Ich gehe mit den andern." [I am going with the others.] I will go my own way, Mr. Dinkel, and not alone: I will be a leader of others.'"

9 THE LION IN WINTER

Not since Julius Caesar himself proclaimed triumph so euphoniously—*veni, vidi, vici*—had any foreigner so conquered another land as Agassiz dazzled America. Ralph Waldo Emerson, later Agassiz's bosom buddy, had proclaimed intellectual independence from Europe in his famous address of 1837: *The American Scholar*. We have, Emerson wrote, "listened too long to the courtly muses of Europe....We will walk on our own feet; we will work with our own hands; we will speak our own minds." But Emerson's sage advice withered before Agassizls charm and intelligence. He was, after all, the first great European theorist in biology who came not to collect and exploit data for the idea mills of European universities and scientific societies but to settle, and to prove thereby that America had come of intellectual age.

Emerson's son described the charm of Agassiz's initial lectures of 1847: "His genial face, his interesting foreign accent, and his facile blackboard drawing, won the game completely.... It was the same with country Lyceum audiences, and in mansion or cottage he won the hearts of his entertainers. Harvard College capitulated the next year. Agassiz was appointed Professor." And Ralph Waldo himself recorded his first impressions of Agassiz in his journal:

> I saw...a broad-featured, unctuous man, fat and plenteous as some successful politician, and pretty soon divined it must be the foreign professor who has had so marked a success in all our scientific and social circles, having established unquestionable leadership in them all; and it was Agassiz.

Louis Agassiz went from triumph to triumph in his adopted land, though his energies focussed on the museum that he opened at Harvard in 1859 as a center for both research and teaching — The Museum of Comparative Zoology (where I work and where all the specimens of this chapter reside today). Yet, as he became both a hero of popular culture and a national focus of power in scientific administration, a familiar story began to play itself out — the transition (in all its linguistic crudity) from Young Turk to old fart. Agassiz never again produced a work of research or an original insight to match his youthful and European achievements (see last chapter) of developing the theory of ice ages and monographing the world's fossil fishes.

Agassiz never stopped dreaming and making plans for research. But his projects either faltered, or served only to fight old battles, long settled to his disadvantage. In 1855, for example, he announced elaborate plans for a lavishly illustrated ten-volume treatise, to be sold by prior subscription with volumes appearing annually, and called *Contributions to the Natural History of the United States*. Agassiz, acutely aware that he had published little original research during his first decade in America, now intended to prove that the old fire (so evident in the last chapter) still burned, and had not been snuffed by his whirlwind of administrative, social, and political activity. He wrote to a friend: "I have tried to make the most of the opportunity this continent has afforded me. Now I shall be on trial for the manner in which I have availed myself to them." With slight defensiveness, he stated to Charles Lyell: these volumes "will show that I have not been idle during ten years' silence."

Agassiz estimated that he would need 450 subscriptions to float his volumes. In May 1855, he launched his plan with usual skill and aplomb, and sent 10,000 copies of promotional material to the bright, the wealthy, and the socially upward bound throughout the world (even commandeering the free franking privileges of the Smithsonian Institution for foreign mail). Agassiz received 2,500 favorable responses. His biographer Edward Lurie writes: "If any literate individual in America or Europe failed to hear of Agassiz and the *Contributions* during the years from 1855 to 1857, it was surely an accident."

Agassiz worked in a frenzy, and the first two volumes appeared on schedule, and to rave reviews, in 1857. (The volumes included a general treatise called "An Essay on Classification," a masterpiece still worth reading today, and a monograph on North American turtles (see photo 92), beautifully illustrated if a bit arcane for most readers.) Noting the correspondence of these volumes with Agassiz's fiftieth birthday, the Saturday Club (a scholars' circle founded by Emerson and Agassiz and including, in the early years, Longfellow, Hawthorne, and Oliver Wendell Holmes), convened to celebrate the publication with a poem by Longfellow. Agassiz, he said, had ventured

> *Into regions yet untrod;*
> *And read what is still unread*
> *In the manuscripts of God.*

But the next two volumes on static taxonomies of invertebrates (primarily of jellyfishes) appeared late, inadequate, and increasingly out of touch with Darwin's new dynamic world.

88. Piranha from the Thayer Expedition

89. Catfish caught by William James, Thayer Expedition

Moreover, most of the technical work had actually been carried out by Agassiz's assistant H. J. Clark—a situation that would fester and later erupt into public bitterness when Clark rebelled and Agassiz attempted to fire him, not only from his Museum but from the Harvard faculty as well. In any case, no further volumes appeared and Agassiz's greatest American project, the salvation of his research life and the resurrection of his professional career, remained but 40 percent complete, with most of the technical work done by someone else.

This same pattern dogged Agassiz's other research forays. He led two highly trumpeted expeditions late in his life—the Thayer Expedition to Brazil (April 1865 to August 1866), and the Hassler Expedition down the coast of South America, through the Straits of Magellan, up to the Galapagos Islands and on to San Francisco (December 1871 to August 1872). Both these expeditions had scientific value, particularly in adding specimens to the collections of Agassiz's museum. The Thayer Expedition, in particular, amassed a wonderful collection of fresh water fishes (see photo 88), as Agassiz hoped to duplicate, at more maturity and greater depth, his first major work as a budding naturalist in Europe—his monograph of Brazilian fishes. Moreover, Agassiz did pursue his acknowledged role as a great teacher. On the Thayer Expedition, he took along six Harvard undergraduate students for instruction and training in natural history—and he gave them endless lectures and practical demonstrations with his usual zeal. One of these six later achieved maximal fame and honor in another, though related, calling—William James (see photo 89 of a fish collected by James on the Thayer Expedition).

But the scientific worth of these exhibits floundered on the realities of Agassiz's changed priorities and commitments as a public man. In a rare moment of candor and self-analysis, he wrote to his friend Lyman: "I am falling behind in my influence among scientific men....I do not write enough, and especially not enough of that stuff which is neither attractive nor instructive to the many, but which might check some of the weak productions with which we are flooded." But Agassiz published essentially nothing for professional colleagues on the scientific results of the two expeditions. (He did write several popular articles for the *Atlantic Monthly* and, in 1868, a travel book with his wife entitled *A Journey to Brazil*—a charming example of a contemporary genre for vicarious pleasure before the age of film, but scarcely a weighty tome.)

Moreover, and especially, Agassiz directed his scientific thoughts to fighting rearguard actions in old battles, lost long ago—particularly in defending his creationism against the Darwinian tide. In Brazil, he mistook evidence of tropical weathering for glacial action and argued that the entire earth had frozen during the last ice age (since glaciers had reached the equator)—thus eliminating all life and requiring a new divine creation for the modern fauna. His old friend Lyell (who had arranged the lectures that originally brought Agassiz to America) wrote:

> Agassiz...has gone wild about glaciers....The whole of
> the great [Amazon] valley, down to its mouth was filled
> with ice....He does not pretend to have met with a single

> glaciated pebble or polished rock . . . . As to the annihilation during the cold of all tropical . . . .plants and animals, that would give no trouble at all to one who can create without scruple not only any number of species at once, but all the separate individuals of a species capable of being supported at one time in their allotted geographical province.

Agassiz hoped that the *Hassler*, outfitted for deep-sea dredging, would disprove evolution by a false argument that only showed his misunderstanding of Darwin. (He wished to bring up, from the "permanently calm" oceanic depths, living representatives of ancient fossil species, spared from the rigors of extinction on land. But Darwin would not have been unhappy with prolonged stability among species in constant environments exerting no pressure of natural selection for change. In any case, the dredging equipment never worked properly and the issue became moot.)

Again, we note the constant and sad disparity between Agassiz's dreams and memories of youthful intellectual vigor, and the realities of his old age. He claimed that he mounted the *Hassler* Expedition in order to approach evolution with an open mind, free from surrounding culture and administrative responsibility. He wrote to his friend, the great German anatomist Carl Gegenbaur:

> I have sailed across the Atlantic Ocean through the Strait of Magellan, and along the western coast of South America to the northern latitudes. Marine animals were, naturally, my primary concern, but I also had a special purpose. I wanted to study the entire Darwinian theory free from all external influences and former surroundings. Was it not on a similar voyage that Darwin developed his present opinions! I took few books with me . . . primarily Darwin's major works.

But Agassiz could no longer see beyond his firm assumptions. He even visited the Galapagos islands on the *Hassler* trip, but saw nothing worth writing down, beyond a specious argument (in a single paragraph) that the islands were too young for their supposed evolutionary changes at Darwinian rates. (Agassiz did see pristine lava flows devoid of vegetation, but many of the islands, including some on his itinerary, are densely vegetated and old enough for any postulated evolution.)

Agassiz's intellectual fossilization centered on his implacable opposition to evolution. For Agassiz could never abandon his truly Platonic view of species and taxonomy: each species is the incarnation of a permanent idea in the mind of God; the relationships among species (taxonomy) therefore provide our most direct insight into the nature of divine thought. All his troubles, his belligerencies, his withdrawal from scientific life, can be traced to this central intransigence. In a telling and most unfortunate episode, in 1863, Agassiz's student assistants, most of whom accepted the new Darwinian excitement (or at least wanted free discussion of the subject), rebelled against the boss's authoritarian policies (no work on personal research during museum hours, no publication without professorial approval). They formed an organization called (only partially in jest) the "Society for the Protection of American Students from Foreign Professors." Agassiz drummed them all out (many became leaders of American natural history at other institutions) and hired, in their stead, old and trusted lackeys and scientists of dependably like mind. Never, in Agassiz's lifetime, did the museum recapture its original intellectual vigor.

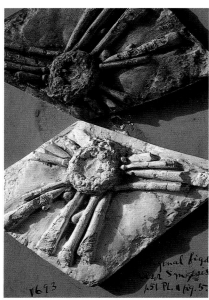

90. Original specimen with cast by Agassiz

Agassiz's last article, published posthumously in the *Atlantic Monthly* in 1874, continued to defend not only creationism in general, but the long disproven taxonomy of Cuvier that formed the foundation of Agassiz's lifelong version. Cuvier divided the animal kingdom into four major branches — vertebrates, mollusks, articulates (segmented worms and arthropods), and radiates (radially symmetrical animals). The first three groups are largely valid, though their interrelationships are genealogical. But the radiates are a false amalgam, largely composed of two disparate groups — the coelenterates (corals and jellyfishes) and the echinoderms (sea urchins and starfishes). The echinoderms are actually close relatives of vertebrates, but Agassiz would never abandon the Radiata — see photo 90 for specimens of echinoderms, collected by Agassiz in Europe during happier days and brought to America. Photo 91 also includes a plaster cast made by Agassiz himself. Agassiz made an important contribution in developing techniques of casting for better resolution of details on counterpart surfaces, and for exchanging good replicas of important specimens among museums.

How shall we judge the later life of this complex, passionate man who was, by far, the most important human force in establishing the science of natural history in nineteenth-century America? Shall we merely lament his intellectual stagnation, or should we broaden our focus, perhaps in the service of a more generous view? In a telling essay published in 1968 (entitled *Thoughts on Research*), the great geneticist Curt Stern, towards the end of his own career, addressed a plea to young scientists in the midst of their initial excitement, competitive vigor, and, yes, ambition. Many older scientists, he wrote, run out of steam for one reason or another, and choose to curtail or abandon original research (Stern never did by the way, and his essay is no *apologia pro vita sua*). Stern writes:

91. Echinoderms

There are some fortunate minds whose fertility gives them an ample supply of new ideas. Yet it is human fate that time passes on, and the river of knowledge is mightier than the mightiest single mind.... It is not surprising that many researchers fall by the wayside.... There are investigators of renown who outlived by decades the period of their accomplishments. Courageously, some men will by an act of decision terminate early or in middle age their search as investigators.... Coolly, they will compute the probability of future research gains and, judging this probability to be low, devote themselves to teaching alone or to administrative tasks. Often their former colleagues look down on them. "He doesn't do any work any more" is a familiar, cruel comment. But why not permit the honesty of the insight that to create is a hazardous undertaking? He who has tried it has also the right to choose a task where, as a teacher, he can re-create knowledge and attitudes, or where, as an administrator, he can apply his thoughts to the prerequisites of research and teaching.

I see two implications, for Agassiz's case, in Stern's insightful and compassionate views. First, if we are to blame Agassiz for anything, we can only lament his personal inability to make Stern's cool computation, and to admit the ravages of time—thus exposing himself to the ridicule of countless promises, never fulfilled, for renewed vigor in research. But these failures can only have been a personal torture for Agassiz; they did not palpably affect the rest of his profession, so why judge him harshly for a pattern that only led to his own distress?

Secondly, Stern advises us to look for other accomplishments in the allied and symbiotic domains of teaching and administration if we wish to judge the continuing importance to science (broadly defined) of people who did distinguished research early in their careers. On these fair grounds, we should put aside Agassiz's later failures in original investigation (a quintessentially private enterprise) and look instead at the public man. We might best view Agassiz's life as composed of two different, sequential parts, each notably successful—the young European researcher, and the older American public spokesman for science (our two chapters on Agassiz follow this proposed division).

As a public man, his successes and his innovations continued. Everyone admired his brilliant and animated lectures. His "hands-on" approach to science, epitomized in his famous motto "study nature, not books," was innovative and challenging. Perhaps the most celebrated tale in nineteenth-century science education, still repeated today, recalls Agassiz's first lesson to the budding naturalist N. S. Shaler. He gave Shaler a single fish, telling him simply to study and to report what he had learned. Whatever Shaler found, Agassiz pointed out aspects overlooked and ordered more careful study of the single specimen itself—no books, no generalities. This procedure continued for two weeks as the fish decayed. When

Shaler discovered an error in Agassiz's own published ideas, the professor replied: "My boy, now there are two of us who know that." Above all, everyone spoke of his boundless energy and enthusiasm, lasting through all illness right to the close of his life. Consider only the testimony of William James, who remained critical of Agassiz's ideas, but came to respect his teaching:

> I have profited a great deal by hearing Agassiz talk, not so much by what he says, for never did a man utter a greater amount of humbug, but by learning the way of feeling of such a vast practical engine as he is . . . . I delight to be with him. I only saw his defects at first, but now his wonderful qualities throw them quite in the background . . . . I never saw a man work so hard.

Agassiz was also an institutional innovator. He favored education in natural history for women (his second wife founded Radcliffe College). In the last year of his life, Agassiz established a coeducational summer school in natural history on Penikese Island— the forerunner to the continuing and highly successful Marine Biological Laboratory at Woods Hole.

Agassiz also delighted in promoting the excitement of natural history beyond the university to lectures in town halls and associations of working men and women. He wrote many books and articles for popular consumption, thus greatly advancing both the prestige and knowledge of natural history. Oliver Wendell Homles was so pleased by Agassiz's efforts that he chose to place "officially" in a letter what he could have told Agassiz in more ephemeral direct conversation:

> I look with ever increasing admiration on the work you are performing for our civilization. It very rarely happens that the same person can take at once the largest and deepest scientific views and come down without apparent effort to the level of popular intelligence. This is what singularly gifts you for our country . . . . You have gained the heart of our purpose; you have taken hold of our understandings by your familiar lectures and writings . . . . I did not think it necessary to say these . . . words, but I wanted the privilege, because I feel them sincerely.

But Agassiz may have had even more impact as an administrator. He held great power, locally and nationally, in the institutions of science. (He was instrumental, for example, in persuading President Lincoln to establish the National Academy of Sciences in 1863.) All his

92. Green sea turtles

skill, his zeal, his intelligence, and his charm came together in promoting—and then building and maintaining—his vision of the key institution in natural history: a great museum that would both display to the public and serve as a national center for research and teaching based on a great collection of specimens, both modern and fossil.

He chose for his institution the odd, but singularly appropriate name: Museum of Comparative Zoology—a title that we still proudly maintain. (Agassiz argued that, in contrast with the experimental procedures of other sciences, natural history must study the uniquenesses of nature's infinite variety. In searching for general principles amidst such irreducible diversity, one must use the "comparative" approach in seeking relationships among clusters of unique objects. To study change through time, compare living and fossil. To study the nature of taxonomic relationships, compare cat with dog and recognize a closer affinity than either with cow.) Ironically, Agassiz's museum opened in 1859, the year of publication for Darwin's *Origin of Species*—the undoing of Agassiz's first life in research. Yet the fruits of his second life in teaching and administration lie before us daily in the great museum that now serves as a center for evolutionary research.

Agassiz sunk all his energy into the Museum. He raised the incredible sum (by standards then prevailing) of $600,000 to support the museum, including direct subsidies of $100,000 (even more incredible, both then and now) from the Massachusetts State Legisla-

93. The "Baron of Orford" no. 1 specimen

94. Claw of *ursus americanus* with bag originally for the bones

ture. Agassiz's zeal in obtaining specimens for the museum collections was legendary, indeed almost maniacal. Any money that came in (including private funds legitimately placeable in his personal bank account) went quickly out to purchase more collections. He drove his son (and eventual successor as museum boss) nearly to distraction as bankruptcy threatened again and again. Alexander Agassiz cried in a letter of frustration to his father's friend Lyman, begging intercession to persuade Louis to put aside some funds as a reserve: "Of course you cannot stop a steam engine going down an inclined plane any more than I can stop father and yet I have to."

Agassiz didn't know the word, but as an indication of his zeal, consider his chutzpah in writing to Secretary of War Edwin M. Stanton in January 1865, when the man presumably had other things on his mind:

> Now that the temperature is low enough...permit me to recall to your memory your promise to let me have the bodies of some Indians; if any should die at this time.... All that would be necessary...would be to forward the body express in a box....Direct the surgeon in charge to inject through the carotids a solution of arsenate of soda. I should like one or two handsome fellows entire and the heads of two or three more.

We are the beneficiaries of this human steam engine. My title is Alexander Agassiz Professor of Zoology (Alex finally made the money that Louis would have spent by running the highly profitable Hecla and Calumet Copper Company). Rosamond found the material for this chapter in the wonderful collections of the Museum of Comparative Zoology. Photo 93 is specimen number one in the catalog of the mammal department—the skull of a famous bull known as the "Baron of Orford." Photo 94, is a back claw of an American brown bear (with each bone neatly numbered), next to a bag of bones labeled "left fore," containing more of the same animal. Photo 95 is an ancestor to the fish collection, a specimen mounted on paper from the Peck Collection of the 1790s (later incorporated by Agassiz into his growing stores).

Edward Lurie, Agassiz's most distinguished modern biographer, once told me that, after writing his major work on the man (*Louis Agassiz, A Life in Science*, University of Chicago Press, 1960), he has been trying to escape him ever since by working on unrelated aspects of nineteenth-century natural history in the United States. But he never succeeds because Agassiz is so central, so pervasive, apparently omnipresent. Work on an obscure amateur collector some-

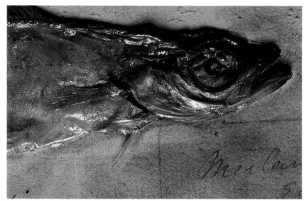

95. Varnished fish on paper

where in Oregon and you find a letter from Agassiz urging the transport of specimens. Study the farmer's benevolent institution of some region in the Great Plains and you discover that Agassiz once gave a crucial lecture in the market town.

I feel much the same way. Agassiz has been dead for nearly 120 years but he is a hovering presence in my world. The Saturday Club still exists; I am a member, and stories of Agassiz and Emerson are still frequently told, as if these great men had merely stepped out on a temporary, if extended, vacation. I was elected to the National Academy of Sciences last year and invited to sign the book of membership. I turned to page one and noted the first signature: Louis Agassiz. A few years ago, we washed down the walls of my office, preparatory to the once-per-generation paint job. We went through a half dozen layers of paint to reveal an original function that I had not suspected. My office had been the central exhibition hall of Agassiz's museum—and the walls were festooned with labels, in lovely Victorian flow, citing Cuvier's creationist classification as a "synopsis of the animal kingdom." (And then, thank God, I didn't have to endure the disruption of painting, for I would never efface this hidden legacy.)

Agassiz has been dead for 120 years, but, to end (as I began) with Julius Caesar, he continues to bestride my world like a colossus.

NOTE: The specimens depicted in "Les Poissons Fossiles" come from the British Museum of Natural History, London. The fossil fish from Lyme Regis comes from the Sedgwick Museum, Cambridge, England. The other specimens come from the Museum of Comparative Zoology, Cambridge, Massachusetts.

PHOTOGRAPHER'S AFTERWORD

As a photographer, I have long been drawn to natural history and anatomical collections. I am intrigued by traditional museum conceits: classification, juxtaposition of words and objects, the relationship of the collectors or curators to their collections, in short, the grey area between a rational scientific system and human idiosyncrasies.

Private and institutional collectors share the same instinctive hunger: to seek, to find, to classify. I've heard of a man in the deep country who has collected furniture, clothes, paper, and arranged them systematically (by class of object) along the road and through a field. He visits his collection daily, checking, sorting, talking, handling every part to be certain nothing is out of place, nothing gone awry. No conscientious collection manager in a big city museum would do otherwise.

I've heard of a bottle collector who had recently realized he had a passion for books. He explained, "I'm digging now, but I'm still shallow," which expresses for me that particular sweet uneasiness which is an essential part of the predator/collector's mind on the prowl. True collectors never touch bottom.

A careful small grouping of fossils and lumps of iron pyrite has been found in a cave in France once inhabited by Neanderthals. The mysterious assemblage, probably made over 35,000 years ago by modern man's distant cousins, appears far removed from serving any practical utilitarian purpose.[1] The instinct for creative personal hoarding seems both ancient and widespread.

Pride of ownership can of course turn a collection into public display. The earliest museum

---

[1] Michel Egloff, "Préhistoire de la collection," *"Collections Passion,"* Neuchâtel: Musée d'ethnographie, 1982), p. 185. The name of the cave is Grotte de l'Hyène à Arcy-sur-Cure (Yonne).

96. Solnhofen shrimp, part/counterpart, Alexander Agassiz, Museum of Comparative Zoology, Harvard

97. *Homo sapiens, Gorilla gorilla,* Ourangutan, Leningrad, Museum of Zoology

98. Human hand (preserved in mercury, Albinus, 18th century), deformed apples, 19th century, apple, 20th century, Leiden

we know about was built in Ur in 550 B.C. by Princess Bel-Shati Nannar and supposedly included a collection of antiques, a foot from a large statue from 2058 B.C., transcriptions of Sumerian texts on tablets, and school children's slates.[2] These are hoarded fragments of historical memory put back—one hopes—into the public domain. The object with the earliest known documentation may be found in the Egyptian museum in Turin—a sea urchin from the Eocene on which is inscribed, in Egyptian hieroglyphs, the date, the name of the collector, and the locality of the find.

In Gulmit, in the northern mountains of Pakistan, a one-room museum houses—among other artifacts—a poorly stuffed snow leopard, a few "dragen bones killed by Babai Gundi," and a weapon, "King Killer used against Fort. Colnel Deene was ingured by this gun." The spirit of the cabinet of curiosities lives on in these natural and ethnographic mementos, part history, part hearsay. I think, in such a barren place, we should accept the "dragen" bones. Facts are fine, but myth is often richer.

Mythical creatures have two possible fates: either they are never found and therefore proved imaginary, or they gradually become real. The unicorn horn ground to produce a miracle

---

[2]Ibid., p. 187.

drug by apothecaries was first reclassified as a narwhal tusk (by Olaus Worm, 1650, among others), and later as the horn of the black rhino. The salamander of mythology which "not only walks through fire, but puts it out in doing so" (Aristotle) and has asbestos for wool, for a long time remained a legend to the Russians. Alexis, father of Peter the Great, wrote from Lebanon in 1697,

> Here I have seen a great marvel which at home they used to
> say was a lie: a man here has in his apothecary's shop in a jar
> of spirits a salamander which I took out and held in my
> own hands. This is word for word exactly as has been
> written.[3]

The salamander, in fact, often found its way into cabinets of curiosities of the sixteenth and seventeenth centuries along with tortoises, alligators, and fishes. The apothecary shop itself seems to be the precursor of private cabinets:

> ...in his needy shop a tortoise hung,
> An alligator stuff'd and other skins
> of ill-shap'd fishes, and about his shelves
> A beggarly account of empty boxes,
> Green earthen pots, bladders and musty seeds,
> Remnants of packthread, and old cakes of roses
> Were thinly scattered to make up a show.
> (*Romeo and Juliet,* V, 1)

Occasionally, actual specimens plainly visible in old plates or listed in the original catalogues reappear on contemporary shelves (Afterward photo 100.). Reconstruction of most of the older cabinets would be, I sadly suspect, a futile exercise. The resurrected artifacts would be as Shakespeare's potpourri, "thinly scattered to make up a show."[4]

Much has decayed, but God only knows what has been thrown away, Fire, war, death, and auctions have broken up collections. Museum personnel may reclassify or discard whatever does not fit in with current trends. Specimens scarce on data are vulnerable; aesthetics, at least in zoological collections, rarely enter into the fate of an unclassified specimen.

---

[3] Arthur MacGregor and Oliver Impey, eds., *The Origin of Museums in the Sixteenth and Seventeenth Centuries* (Oxford University Press, 1984).

[4] Actual reconstructions or exhibitions I have either seen or heard about include the Tradescant Room at the University Museum, Oxford, The Anatomisch Theatre, Leiden (1991), the Cabinet of Settalla, Milan (1989), and a reconstruction of the room of Olaus Worm in Copenhagen (1990). I am grateful to the essay by Wilma George in *The Origins of Museums in the Sixteenth and Seventeeth Centuries*, in which the connection between the apothecary's shop and early cabinets is drawn.

99. Owls from collection of blind ornithologist, van Wickevoort-Krommelin, Leiden

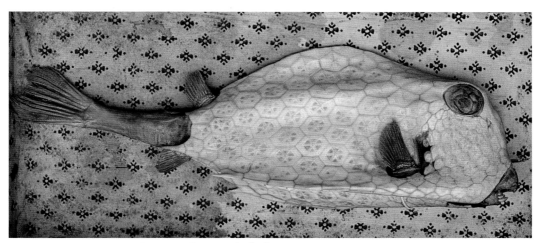

100. Trunkfish from Tradescant collection, Oxford

Part of the pleasure of viewing older collections comes from not knowing exactly what to expect. Take Leningrad, where, for my benefit, after tea, the collection manager took his raincoat off the mirror, took the mirror off the hook, unlocked the closet door behind, and produced, in order, a lock of Peter the Great's hair, a list of his dental patients, the death mask of Charles XII (all reproduced herein), and a particularly sensational part of the giant Bourgeois.

These artifacts are as full of human lunacy and gravity as any collector of oddities could wish for. But why these things and not others? None of them are particularly attractive or intrinsically valuable. Princess Dashkoff, who, under Catherine the Great, ruthlessly discarded so much of Peter's collection, somehow overlooked these bits. They escaped Dashkoff, they escaped institutional upheavals, and they slipped through all the wars. There is a random quality to collections that come down through time, and we see the true survivors. I think of the children in alcohol as having come to us in a time capsule. I, for one, had never seen the eyes of a person who lived in the seventeeth century until I saw the girl with the lace collar.

For all this talk of fragmentation, most collections are so vast that it would take a lot more than the brief flitting by of one photographer to render properly aesthetic justice. However, "the camera is the ideal arm of consciousness in its acquisitive mood" (Susan Sontag).

So where does one begin? The boxes and boxes of van Heurn's somewhat macabre, perfectly pressed skins of rabbits, rats, dogs, cats, pigs, and moles, coupled with his ideas about order and taxonomy, caught my attention long before we began to work on this book. He seemed to me to be a kind of a "black hole" collector, insatiable and a bit out of control. He had to have it all.

My favorite collector must be the one who is almost not here—Mary Anning, whose shrewd intensity shows as she closes a letter: "... The tide warns me, I must leave a

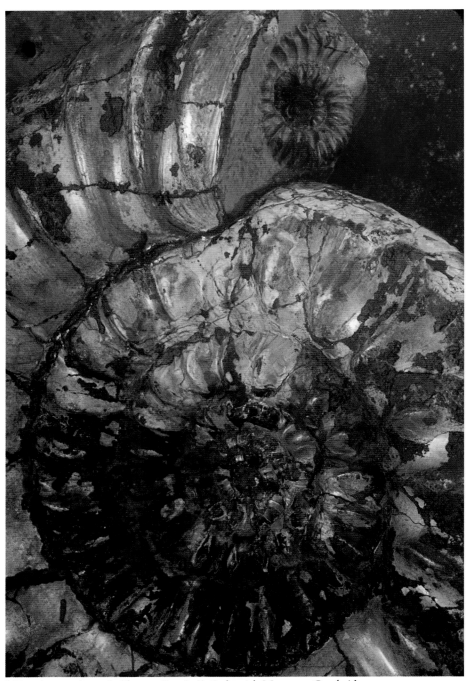

101. Ammonite sealed by smaller shell, Sedgwick Museum, Cambridge

102. Slice of ammonites, University Museum, Oxford

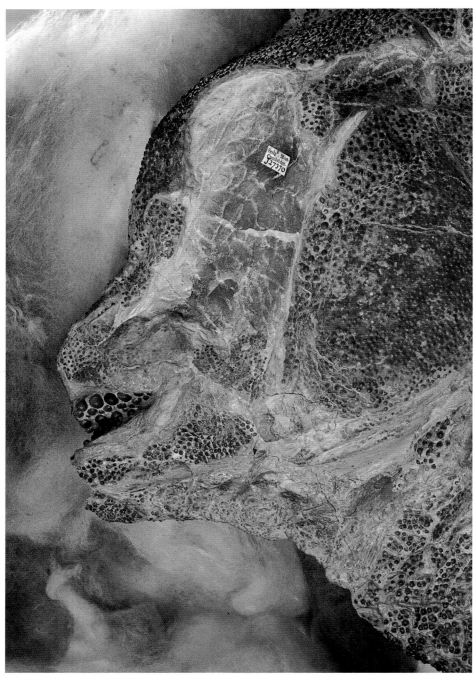

103. Head of fossil fish, Sedgwick Museum, Cambridge

104. Hedgehogs, porcupines, echidna, Leiden

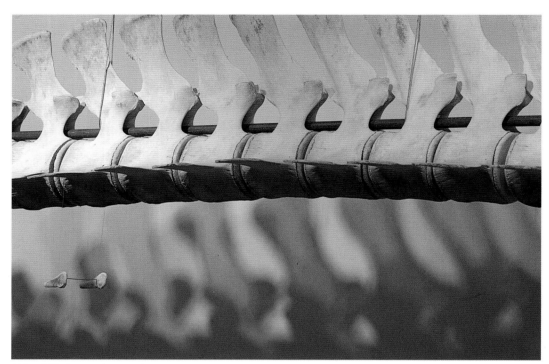

105. Whale vertebrae and pelvis, Leiden

scribilling."[5] Better not lose that next ichthyosaur. No keeper she, and free, therefore, to go forth to seek fresh treasure.

It gave me great satisfaction to match the fossils found by Scilla to his intricate drawings (and to find the fossils coarser than the art), to arrange the Birds of Paradise hour after hour, and to have a particularly ponderous ichthyosaur hoisted to the ground for my pleasure by three men and a fork lift.

Although I photograph everything just slightly out of context (fossil on a wooden chair, pigs on the floor, only parts of the ichthyosaurs), I tried as much as possible not to add inappropriate detail. Once seen, however, it is hard to separate the cigar box from the brain cast (see Dubois); it is difficult to ignore blue-bleached cotton when it appears in the vicinity of a fossil shark tooth (see Scilla). I used a piece of scratched metal with Agassiz's bear claw and instinctively propped the Baron of Orford (see Agassiz) on the upper jaw of a nearby sperm whale. My rule is to use whatever comes spontaneously to hand.

The animals don't move, but the light moves, the best light is brief and the collection manager is often rustling in the wings. The tide warns me. Vita brevis, sweet life.

---

[5]Anning to J. S. Miller, Bristol Institution, 1830.

106. Saki, golden lion tamarin, Leiden

ACKNOWLEDGEMENTS

I thank all the curators, collection managers, and keepers who tolerated my presence in their collection.

In Leiden, at the Rijksmuseum of Natuurliche Historie, I thank Dr. L. B. Holthuis, Dr. G. V. F. Mees, Dr. Chris Smeenck, Dr. John De Vos, and Rob Vroom, and at the Anatomische Museum, Willem Mulder and Dr. Elshout-Lehendijk.

In Leningrad, at the N. N. Miklukho-Maklay Institute, I am especially indebted to the director, Dr. Rudolph Itz, Dr. Anna Radzun, Dr. A. G. Kozintsev, Vladimir Kislyakov, and Nina Klimova, and at the Zoology Museum in Leningrad, Dr. Roald Patapov.

At the American Museum of Natural History, I am very grateful to Dr. Mary Lecroy for sharing her wisdom along with Rothschild's Birds of Paradise.

At the Museum of Comparative Zoology at Harvard, I thank the Director, James McCarthy, Maria Rutzmoser, Jane Harrison, Amy Davidson, Judy Chupasko, Dr. Karsten Hartel, Jennifer Bush, Jose Rosado, Ron Eng, Felicita d'Escrivan, Dr. Stephen Gould (here as Curator), and especially Agnes Pilot, who helps and helps.

At the University Museum, Oxford, I am especially grateful to Phil Powell and Jane Pickering. At the Sedgwick Museum, Cambridge, I thank Dr. David Price, Mike Dorling, and Rodrick Long.

At the British Museum of Natural History, I thank Dr. Colin Patterson, Peter Forey, and Alison Longbottom, who kindly put up with two visits to the same six fossils along with what must have seemed like endless diversionary tactics. A good collection is hard to leave behind...

I thank my friends: Dr. William Bennett for his expert translation from the Russian of the history of the Kunstkammer of Peter the Great, Dr. Diana Fane, Dr. Harriet Ritvo, Dr. Laurie Godfrey, and Dr. Melanie Stiassny, for helping me through the thickets of museum and collector lore to the "right words." From a fellowship year at the Bunting Institute, Radcliffe College, I thank Dr. Elisabeth McKinsey, Dr. Ann Bookman, Dr. Michelle Scott, Dr. Heather Dubrow, Wendy Kaminer, Fae Ng, and Rikki Ducornet for all their encouragement.

I treasure conversations about collectors with Mary Wolff, Shelby Lee Adams, Dr. Pere Alberch, William Crawford, M. Hermensader, Dr. Eugenia Janis, Don Lessem, Barbara Pope, Robert and Barbara Wheaton, Roger Swain, Rebecca Nemser, and W. Snyder Mac-Neil. I thank Laura Baring-Gould for ably assisting with many logistical crises. I deeply value all the technical support received over the last three years from Carmen Denato and Jim Rohan at Positive Photographics, Rowena Otremba at Zona Inc., and Anne Doherty, all printers extraordinaires. Love and thanks to Dennis, Andrew, and John Henry Purcell for their advice and support.

I am indebted and very grateful to Pioneer Travel (Arlngton, Mass.), OASIS (Cambridge, Mass.), and to Armen Dedekian, for their work as couriers, travel agents, and advisers for the trip to the Soviet Union. Without their interest and advice, there would have been no photographs from Leningrad.

107. Slice of ammonites, University Museum, Oxford

Technical note:

The photographs in this book were taken with a Nikon FE2,

using 28, 55, and 105 macro lenses. All were

taken with Fujichrome ASA 100, in natural light.